Houghton Mifflin Harcourt

ALGEBRA 2

Getting Ready for High-Stakes Assessment

Printed in the U.S.A.

ISBN   978-1-328-93856-5
1 2 3 4 5 6 7 8 9 10   0928   26 25 24 23 22 21 20 19 18 17
4500668544   A B C D E F G

Contents

Perform arithmetic operations on polynomials.

Understand the relationship between zeros and factors of polynomials.

Use polynomial identities to solve problems.

Rewrite rational expressions.

Create equations that describe numbers or relationships.

Understand solving equations as a process of reasoning and explain the reasoning.

Solve equations and inequalities in one variable.

Solve systems of equations.

Represent and solve equations and inequalities graphically.

Functions and Modeling

Interpret functions that arise in applications in terms of a context.

Analyze functions using different representations.

Build a function that models a relationship between two quantities.

Build new functions from existing functions.

The student will solve $f(x) = c$ for a simple function f that has an inverse and write an expression for the inverse.

Construct and compare linear, quadratic, and exponential models and solve problems.

The student will express as a logarithm the solution to $ab^{ct} = d$, if the base b is 2, 10, or e, and evaluate the logarithm.

Interpret expressions for functions in terms of the situation they model.

The student will interpret the parameters in a linear or exponential function in terms of a context.

Trigonometry

Extend the domain of trigonometric functions using the unit circle.

The student will understand radian measure as the length of the arc on the unit circle subtended by an angle.

The student will explain how the unit circle in the coordinate plane enables the extension of trigonometric functions.

Model periodic phenomena with trigonometric functions.

The student will choose trigonometric functions to model periodic phenomena.

Prove and apply trigonometric identities.

The student will prove the Pythagorean identity $\sin^2(\theta) + \cos^2(\theta) = 1$ and use it to find $\sin(\theta)$, $\cos(\theta)$, or $\tan(\theta)$.

Geometry

Translate between the geometric description and the equation for a conic section.

The student will derive the equation of a parabola given a focus and directrix.

Statistics and Modeling

Summarize, represent, and interpret data on a single count or measurement variable.

The student will use mean and standard deviation to fit data to a normal distribution and to estimate percentages.

Understand and evaluate random processes underlying statistical experiments.

The student will understand statistics as a process for making inferences based on a random sample.

Make inferences and justify conclusions from sample surveys, experiments, and observational studies.

Probability

Understand independence and conditional probability and use them to interpret data.

Use the rules of probability to compute probabilities of compound events in a uniform probability model.

Use probability to evaluate outcomes of decisions.

Some of the items in the practice tests listed in the Contents also involve one or more of the following math processes and practices.

Math Processes and Practices

MPP1	Problem Solving
MPP2	Abstract and Quantitative Reasoning
MPP3	Using and Evaluating Logical Reasoning
MPP4	Mathematical Modeling
MPP5	Using Mathematical Tools
MPP6	Using Precise Mathematical Language
MPP7	Seeing Structure
MPP8	Generalizing

Preparing for High-Stakes Assessments

Your school district or state department of education may require you to take a test that is used to make important decisions, such as which students are eligible for a high school diploma or which teachers are rated as effective. Such tests are commonly called high-stakes assessments.

This *Getting Ready for High-Stakes Assessment* book provides opportunities to prepare for such tests based on what you learn in the math course you're taking. The following tables describe the types of assessment items in this book. Because you may be required to take a test online, the tables also explain how your online experience may differ from the way you complete the practice items in this book.

Each practice test consists of two broad categories of items: selected response and constructed response. Selected response items require you to make one or more choices from a group of options. Constructed response items require you to produce an answer on your own.

Type of Item in *Getting Ready for High-Stakes Assessment*	What Your Online Experience May Be Like

Multiple Choice (a type of selected response): You select the only correct answer from a list of answer choices.
 	
 Example:
 	
 Select the correct answer.
 1. What does the imaginary number *i* represent?
     Ⓐ −1
     Ⓑ $\sqrt{1}$
     Ⓒ $\sqrt{-1}$
     Ⓓ $-\sqrt{-1}$
	On a practice test in this book, you would fill in the oval containing the letter of the answer choice you select. For an online test, you would likely be presented with small circles (sometimes called "radio buttons"). Clicking on one of the circles causes the circle to be filled in.

Type of Item in *Getting Ready for High-Stakes Assessment*	What Your Online Experience May Be Like
Inline Multiple Choice (a type of selected response): This is a variation of Multiple Choice. Here, you make your selection from a list that appears within a sentence. Examples:	On a practice test in this book, you would circle the answer choice that makes a true statement. For an online test, you would likely be presented with a drop-down menu labeled "Choose..." or "Select One." Clicking on the menu displays a list of answer choices. You would then click on the answer choice you want to select.

1. Circle the ordered pair that makes a true statement.

   $\triangle ABC$ is shown below. Suppose the triangle is translated 5 units to the right and 7 units down. The coordinates of the image of vertex C after this

   transformation are
   | $(-8, -6)$ |
   | $(2, -6)$ |
   | $(-3, -6)$ |
   | $(2, 0)$ |
   .

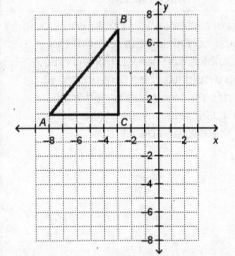

Type of Item in *Getting Ready for High-Stakes Assessment*	What Your Online Experience May Be Like

Multiple Response (a type of selected response): You select all correct answers from a list of possible answers.
 	
Examples:
 	
Select all correct answers.
3. Consider the directed line segment from $M(-3, 1)$ to $N(3, 4)$. Determine which of the following statements are true.
  (A) The point $P(1, 3)$ partitions the segment in the ratio 2 to 1.
  (B) The point $Q(-1, 2)$ partitions the segment in the ratio 1 to 2.
  (C) The point $R(0, 2.5)$ partitions the segment in the ratio 1 to 2.
  (D) The point $S(0, 2.5)$ partitions the segment in the ratio 1 to 1.
  (E) The point $T(-1, 4.5)$ partitions the segment in the ratio 1 to 1.
 	
4. Circle each expression that is equal to $\left(p^{-3}\right)^{\frac{2}{5}}$. Assume that p is positive.
 	
  $\sqrt[5]{p^{-6}}$ $\sqrt[5]{p^{-13}}$
 	
  $\dfrac{1}{\sqrt{p^{15}}}$ $\dfrac{1}{p\sqrt[5]{p}}$
 	
  $\dfrac{1}{p^{30}}$ $\sqrt[10]{p^{-1}}$
	On a practice test in this book, you would make selections by filling in ovals or circling answer choices. For an online test, you might be presented with "hot spots." The "hot spots" are boxes containing answer choices that light up when you click on them. Alternatively, each answer choice might have a small square next to it. Clicking the squares causes check marks to appear in them to indicate that you have selected those answer choices.

Type of Item in *Getting Ready for High-Stakes Assessment*	What Your Online Experience May Be Like
Categorization (a type of selected response): You assign given objects to categories by making a series of Yes/No, True/False, or Category A/Category B choices. Sometimes there may be more than two categories, such as True/False/Cannot Be Determined.	On a practice test in this book, you would put a check mark in the appropriate column for the given object in each row of a table. For an online test, each cell of the table might have a small square that displays a check mark when you click on it. Alternatively, each cell might have a small circle that fills in when you click on it.

Examples:

4. Consider the function $f(x) = 2x^2 + 4x - 30$. Indicate whether each statement is true of false by putting a check mark in the appropriate column of the table.

	True	False
The vertex of the graph is (1, −32).		
The zeros are 3 and −5.		
The graph opens down.		
The axis of symmetry is $x = -1$.		
The y-intercept is −30.		

5. Indicate whether each of the following is rational or irrational by putting a check mark in the appropriate column of the table.

	Rational	Irrational
The product of $\sqrt{2}$ and 5		
$f(x) = x^2 + 2$ evaluated at $x = \sqrt{7}$		
The sum of $\sqrt{10}$ and $\sqrt{16}$		
$f(r) = \pi r^2$ evaluated at $r = 3$		

Type of Item in *Getting Ready for High-Stakes Assessment*	What Your Online Experience May Be Like
Matching (a type of selected response): You match an answer choice with each given object. Examples:	On a practice test in this book, you would write either the letter of an answer choice or the answer choice itself next to each given object. For an online test, you might use drag and drop to move an answer choice next to each given object. Alternatively, you might click on both a given object and an answer choice to link them as a match.

Match each equation with the description of the circle it represents.

_____ 4. $(x-4)^2 + (y-5)^2 = 4$

_____ 5. $(x+7)^2 + (y-2)^2 = 9$

_____ 6. $x^2 - 10x + y^2 - 8y = -39$

_____ 7. $x^2 + 8x + y^2 + 10y = -25$

_____ 8. $x^2 - 4x + y^2 + 14y = -50$

A center: $(-7, 2)$; radius 3

B center: $(-7, -2)$; radius $\sqrt{3}$

C center: $(-2, 7)$; radius 3

D center: $(2, -7)$; radius $\sqrt{3}$

E center: $(-4, -5)$; radius 4

F center: $(4, 5)$; radius 2

G center: $(5, -4)$; radius $\sqrt{2}$

H center: $(5, 4)$; radius $\sqrt{2}$

Match each number with its equivalent form.

Using the list of numbers at the right, write the equivalent form of each given number.

4. $-\sqrt{8}$ [ ]

5. $\sqrt{-8^2}$ [ ]

6. $\sqrt[3]{-8}$ [ ]

7. $\sqrt{-8}$ [ ]

8. $\sqrt{-800}$ [ ]

-8
-2
$-2\sqrt{2}$
$-20\sqrt{2}$
$-2i$
$8i$
$2i\sqrt{2}$
$20i\sqrt{2}$

Type of Item in *Getting Ready for High-Stakes Assessment*	What Your Online Experience May Be Like
Numerical/Algebraic Response (a type of constructed response): You produce a numerical or algebraic answer. Example: 11. a. Find sin *A* in the triangle below. 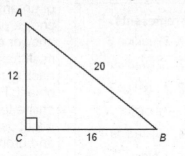 _____ b. Write a different trigonometric ratio with the same value as sin *A*. _____ 4. Find the inverse of $f(x) = \frac{1}{2}\sqrt[3]{x+4} - 5$. Show your work. _____ _____ _____ _____ _____	On a practice test in this book, you write your answer, and you may be asked to show your work, explain your reasoning, or draw a conclusion from your answer. For an online test, you would likely be presented with an input box where you type your answer. If the answer requires the use of mathematical symbols or formatting not available on a computer keyboard, the input box would be accompanied by a palette of symbols and formatting templates that you can use as you type your answer. For a simple input box, you would type just the answer and not show work, explain reasoning, or draw a conclusion.

Type of Item in *Getting Ready for High-Stakes Assessment*	What Your Online Experience May Be Like
Graphical Response (a type of constructed response): You create some type of drawing, such as a function's graph, a data display, or a geometric figure. Examples: 5. Julius is flying home to Los Angeles from Boston. His distance away from home in miles d can be expressed in terms of t hours by the equation $d = 2600 - 500t$. Graph Julius's distance away from home in miles d after t hours, choosing appropriate scales. 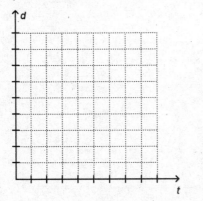 5. The data below are the average annual starting salaries (in thousands of dollars) of 20 randomly selected college graduates. Make a dot plot of the data values. 42 37 40 37 45 39 43 47 36 34 40 43 42 40 37 44 36 46 39 35 	On a practice test in this book, you draw by hand using the provided number line, coordinate plane, or starting figure. For an online test, there are a variety of ways to create drawings depending on the type of drawing: • For graphs that consist of isolated points on a number line or coordinate plane, you might plot the points simply by clicking on the number line or coordinate plane. • For more sophisticated graphs, you might use drawing tools, such as a line-drawing tool that requires you to click on two points in a coordinate plane, with the tool automatically drawing the line through those points. • For geometric figures such as polygons, you might use a connect-consecutive-points tool that automatically draws a line segment between the last point clicked and the next point clicked. • For bar graphs and histograms, you might be given bars with, say, a height of 1, and you adjust the height of a bar by clicking on the top of the bar and dragging either up or down.

Type of Item in *Getting Ready for High-Stakes Assessment*	What Your Online Experience May Be Like
Extended Response/Performance Task (a type of constructed response): You solve a multistep problem. Examples:	On a practice test in this book, you write your answers to lettered parts of a problem, and in at least one of the parts you are asked to show your work, explain your reasoning, or draw conclusions from your answers. For an online test, you would likely be presented with one or more large response boxes. A response box allows to you type lengthy answers and may come with options for formatting text and inserting mathematical symbols.

8. A picture frame hangs on a wall as shown. The wall is 22 feet wide and 9 feet high. The square picture is 6 feet wide and its left corner is 2 feet to the right of the centerline of the wall.

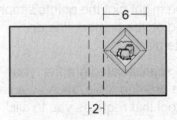

├─ 6 ─┤

├2┤

a. Suppose the lower-left corner of the wall is (0, 0) and the centerline of the wall is the line $x = 11$. Give the coordinates of the corners of the picture frame.

_____

b. You want to locate a congruent picture frame on the left so that the two picture frames will be symmetric across the centerline of the wall. What transformation can you apply to the first picture frame to locate the second picture frame?

_____

c. Give the coordinates of the corners of the second picture frame.

_____

d. Describe a transformation rule using coordinate notation for a reflection across $x = 11$, the centerline of the wall. Explain how you find the transformation rule and confirm it by showing how the rule affects the four corners of the first picture frame.
$(x, y) \rightarrow (?, ?)$

_____

_____

_____

_____

The student will extend properties of integer exponents to rational exponents and write radicals as rational exponents.

SELECTED RESPONSE
Select the correct answer.

1. Write the radical expression in rational exponent form.
   $\sqrt[5]{a}$

   (A) a^5

   (B) $a^{\frac{1}{5}}$

   (C) 5^a

   (D) $\left(\dfrac{1}{5}\right)^a$

2. Write the radical expression in rational exponent form.
   $\sqrt[3]{k^7}$

   (A) $k^{\frac{7}{3}}$

   (B) $k^{\frac{3}{7}}$

   (C) k^4

   (D) k^{10}

3. Circle the inequality that makes a true statement.
   The values of p that result in real numbers when the expression $p^{\frac{3}{2}}$ is evaluated are $\boxed{\begin{array}{l} p \geq 3 \\ p \leq 2 \\ p \leq 0 \\ p \geq 0 \end{array}}$.

Select all correct answers.

4. Which of the following do not have integer exponents when rewritten in rational exponent form and simplified? Assume that s is nonnegative.

   (A) $\sqrt{s^4}$

   (B) $\sqrt[6]{s^3}$

   (C) $\sqrt[4]{s^6}$

   (D) $\sqrt[3]{s^9}$

   (E) $\sqrt[5]{s^{15}}$

   (F) $\sqrt[8]{s^2}$

Match each radical expression with its equivalent rational exponent expression. Assume that w is nonnegative.

____ 5. $\sqrt[3]{w^5}$

____ 6. $\sqrt[5]{w^3}$

____ 7. $\sqrt{w^5}$

____ 8. $\sqrt[3]{w}$

A $w^{\frac{5}{3}}$

B $w^{\frac{3}{5}}$

C $w^{\frac{1}{5}}$

D $w^{\frac{1}{3}}$

E $w^{\frac{2}{5}}$

F $w^{\frac{2}{3}}$

G $w^{\frac{5}{2}}$

H $w^{\frac{3}{2}}$

CONSTRUCTED RESPONSE

9. Given that the fourth root of x is defined as a quantity that, when raised to the fourth power, equals x, explain why it makes sense that $\sqrt[4]{b} = b^{\frac{1}{4}}$.

_____

_____

_____

_____

_____

10. Let $n = 4m$. Rewrite $\sqrt[3n]{a^{2m}}$ in rational exponent form and simplify. Assume that m is positive.

_____

_____

_____

_____

11. Given that the definition of the cube root of x is that it's a quantity that, when raised to the third power, equals x, explain why it makes sense that $\sqrt[3]{x^4} = x^{\frac{4}{3}}$.

_____

_____

_____

_____

12. A student wrote the following:
$$\sqrt[4]{x^2} = x^{\frac{2}{4}} = x^{\frac{1}{2}} = \sqrt{x}$$

Based on this, the student claims that $\sqrt[4]{x^2} = \sqrt{x}$ for all values of x.

a. Give an example of a value of x that makes this statement untrue and explain your reasoning.

_____

_____

_____

_____

_____

_____

_____

_____

_____

_____

_____

b. Explain how you can restrict the value of x so that the student's statement is true.

_____

_____

_____

_____

_____

_____

Name _____ Date _____ Class_____

The student will rewrite expressions involving radicals and rational exponents using the properties of exponents.

SELECTED RESPONSE
Select the correct answer.

1. Simplify $\left(\sqrt[7]{z^3}\right)^8$. Assume z is positive.

   (A) $z^{\frac{56}{3}}$

   (B) $z^{\frac{24}{7}}$

   (C) $z^{\frac{24}{56}}$

   (D) $z^{\frac{11}{15}}$

2. Which of the following is equal to $\sqrt[15]{\left(j^{-3}\right)^{-2}}$? Assume that j is positive.

   (A) $j^{-\frac{2}{5}}$

   (B) $j^{-\frac{1}{3}}$

   (C) $j^{\frac{5}{2}}$

   (D) $j^{\frac{2}{5}}$

3. Write $\left(\sqrt{uv^3}\right)^5$ using rational exponents. Assume u and v are both positive.

   (A) $u^{\frac{5}{2}}v^{\frac{15}{2}}$ (C) $u^{\frac{2}{5}}v^{\frac{2}{15}}$

   (B) u^5v^{15} (D) $u^{\frac{11}{2}}v^{\frac{13}{2}}$

Select all correct answers.

4. Circle each expression that is equal to $\left(p^{-3}\right)^{\frac{2}{5}}$. Assume that p is positive.

   $\sqrt[5]{p^{-6}}$ $\sqrt[5]{p^{-13}}$

   $\dfrac{1}{\sqrt{p^{15}}}$ $\dfrac{1}{p\sqrt[5]{p}}$

   $\dfrac{1}{p^{30}}$ $\sqrt[10]{p^{-1}}$

CONSTRUCTED RESPONSE

5. Write $\left(c^{-9}d^{12}\right)^{-\frac{5}{6}}$ using only positive exponents. Assume c and d are both positive. Show all work.

   _____

   _____

   _____

   _____

   _____

   _____

6. Write the four expressions in descending order of resulting exponent when written in simplified rational exponent form. Assume t is positive.

   $\sqrt[6]{t} \cdot \sqrt[8]{t}$ $\dfrac{t}{t^{\frac{5}{7}}}$ $\left(\sqrt[3]{t^2}\right)^{\frac{4}{7}}$ $\dfrac{1}{t^{-\frac{2}{5}}}$

   _____

   _____

   _____

   _____

   _____

   _____

   _____

   _____

   _____

7. Which values of d give the expression

$$\left[\left(d^{\frac{1}{3}}\right)^{\frac{1}{7}}\right]^{\frac{1}{4}}$$ a real number result when

simplified? Explain your answer.

_____

_____

_____

_____

_____

_____

_____

_____

_____

8. Show that $\left(a^{-\frac{1}{m}}\right)^{-\frac{1}{n}} = \sqrt[mn]{a}$ for positive

values of m, n, and a. Then use this

information to simplify $\left[\left(jk^4\right)^{-\frac{1}{5}}\right]^{-\frac{1}{3}}$ for

positive values of j and k. Show all
work.

_____

_____

_____

_____

_____

_____

9. On a recent exam, Terrell was asked to

simplify $\dfrac{x^{\frac{1}{3}}}{x^{\frac{2}{5}}}$, assuming that x is not

zero. His work is shown below.

$$\frac{x^{\frac{1}{3}}}{x^{\frac{2}{5}}} = x^{\frac{1}{3} \div \frac{2}{5}}$$

$$= x^{\frac{1}{3} \cdot \frac{5}{2}}$$

$$= x^{\frac{5}{6}}$$

$$= \sqrt[6]{x^5}$$

a. What mistake did Terrell make?

_____

_____

_____

_____

b. Find the correct answer. Show your
work.

_____

_____

_____

_____

c. Are the original expression and the
expression you found in part b
equivalent when x is negative?
Explain why or why not. (Hint:
Check to see if both expressions
have real number results with
negative x.)

_____

_____

_____

_____

The student will define appropriate quantities for the purpose of descriptive modeling.

SELECTED RESPONSE

Select the correct answer.

1. Circle the expression that makes a true statement.

   Samantha drove her car for 15 miles at a certain speed s to get to her first destination. She then drove 3 miles less and 10 miles per hour faster to get to her second destination. The expression that models the combined time Samantha spent driving is given by

   $$\frac{15}{s} + \frac{12}{s+10}$$

   $$\frac{15}{s+10} + \frac{12}{s}$$

   $$\frac{15}{s} - \frac{12}{s+10}$$

   $$\frac{s}{15} + \frac{s+10}{12}$$

2. James, Christina, and Miguel rode the Ferris wheel at a carnival. They want to create a mathematical model that would give their height above the ground at any time during the ride. Identify the dependent and independent variables, and choose an appropriate type of function to model the situation.

   (A) The dependent variable is time t. The independent variable is height h. A quadratic function would be the best model for this situation.

   (B) The dependent variable is height h. The independent variable is time t. A quadratic function would be the best model for this situation.

   (C) The dependent variable is height h. The independent variable is time t. A trigonometric function would be the best model for this situation.

   (D) The dependent variable is time t. The independent variable is height h. A trigonometric function would be the best model for this situation.

Select all correct answers.

3. The half-life of a certain radioactive isotope is 3 days. You want to write an exponential expression for the percent of a sample of the isotope that remains after a certain number of days. Which correctly describe the dependent and independent variables in this situation?

   (A) The dependent variable is the remaining percent of the sample, p.

   (B) The independent variable is the remaining percent of the sample, p.

   (C) The independent variable is time t, in days.

   (D) The dependent variable is time t, in days.

   (E) The dependent variable is the mass of the sample, m.

CONSTRUCTED RESPONSE

4. A traffic engineer is modeling the traffic on a highway during the morning commute. The average number of cars on the highway at both 6 a.m. and 10 a.m. is 4000. However, the number of cars is greater than 4000 between 6 a.m. and 10 a.m., reaching a peak of 6500 cars at 8 a.m.

   a. Choose mathematical variables to represent the real-world variables in this situation. Tell which is the independent variable and which is the dependent variable.

   _____

   _____

   b. Write a function of the form $f(x) = a(x - h)^2 + k$, where (h, k) is the vertex of the parabola that models the number of cars on the highway at any time between 6 a.m. and 10 a.m. Explain your reasoning.

   _____

   _____

5. You want to make an open-top box from the rectangular piece of cardboard shown. You cut congruent squares from the four corners of the cardboard and then fold up and tape the resulting flaps.

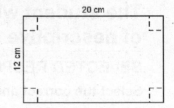

a. Suppose you want to know the volume of the box. Describe the real-world variable on which the volume depends. Then choose a mathematical variable to represent the real-world variable and label the diagram with it.

_____

b. Explain how to find the width, length, and height of the box using the variable from part a.

_____

c. Write an equation that gives the volume V of the box as a function of the variable from part a.

_____

6. While researching the heights of tables and chairs for children, you come across the following table of data. You want to model the data using appropriate functions obtained through the regression feature on a graphing calculator.

Age of Child	Chair Seat Height	Table Top Height
1 year old	5 to 7 inches	12 to 14 inches
2 years old	8 to 10 inches	16 to 18 inches
3 years old	10 inches	18 inches
4 years old	10 to 12 inches	18 to 20 inches
5 years old	12 inches	20 inches
6 years old	12 to 14 inches	20 to 22 inches
7 years old	13 to 14 inches	21 to 22 inches
8 years old	14 to 15 inches	22 to 25 inches
9 years old	14 to 16 inches	22 to 26 inches
10 years old	16 inches	24 to 26 inches
11 years old	16 to 17 inches	24 to 27 inches
12 years old	16 to 18 inches	24 to 29 inches
13 years old and up	18 inches	26 to 30 inches

a. Identify the three real-world variables given in the table and choose an appropriate mathematical variable to represent each. Include the unit of measurement for each defined variable.

_____

b. For each model you want to create, describe which variable is the independent variable and which is the dependent variable. Explain your reasoning.

_____

c. When you enter the data in your calculator, describe what you will do with heights given as ranges (such as a chair seat height of 5 to 7 inches for 1-year-olds). Explain your reasoning.

_____

The student will know there is a complex number i such that $i^2 = -1$, and every complex number has the form $a + bi$.

SELECTED RESPONSE

Select the correct answer.

1. What does the imaginary number i represent?

   (A) -1

   (B) $\sqrt{1}$

   (C) $\sqrt{-1}$

   (D) $-\sqrt{-1}$

2. Which of the following is equivalent to $\sqrt{-121}$?

   (A) 11

   (B) -11

   (C) $11i$

   (D) $121i$

Select all correct answers.

3. Find all solutions of the equation $x^2 = -484$.

   (A) $x = 22$

   (B) $x = -22$

   (C) $x = 22i$

   (D) $x = -22i$

Match each number with its equivalent form.

Using the list of numbers at the right, write the equivalent form of each given number.

4. $-\sqrt{8}$ [____]

5. $\sqrt{-8^2}$ [____]

6. $\sqrt[3]{-8}$ [____]

7. $\sqrt{-8}$ [____]

8. $\sqrt{-800}$ [____]

-8
-2
$-2\sqrt{2}$
$-20\sqrt{2}$
$-2i$
$8i$
$2i\sqrt{2}$
$20i\sqrt{2}$

CONSTRUCTED RESPONSE

9. How many real solutions does the equation $x^4 - 16 = 0$ have? How many non-real solutions? State all solution(s) of the equation.

   _____

   _____

   _____

10. Simplify each expression and tell whether it represents a real number or a non-real number.

    a. $\sqrt{144} - \sqrt{64}$

    _____

    _____

    b. $\sqrt{144} + \sqrt{-64}$.

    _____

    _____

11. How many real solutions and how many non-real solutions does the equation $x^2 + 5 = 0$ have? Describe what implications your answer has for graphing the function $y = x^2 + 5$.

    _____

    _____

    _____

12. Why is it imprecise to say that the equation $25x^2 + 27 = 0$ has no solution? Find all solutions of the equation.

    _____

    _____

    _____

13. Consider the set of real numbers and the set of complex numbers.

   a. Is every real number also a complex number? Explain.

   _____

   _____

   b. Is every complex number also a real number? Explain.

   _____

   _____

   c. Which Venn diagram below accurately represents the two sets of numbers? Explain.

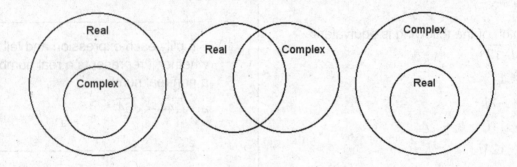

   _____

   _____

The student will use $i^2 = -1$ and number properties to add, subtract, and multiply complex numbers.

SELECTED RESPONSE

Select the correct answer.

1. Let a, b, and c be any real numbers. Find the product $ci(a + bi)$.

   Ⓐ $ac + bci$

   Ⓑ $bc + aci$

   Ⓒ $-bc + aci$

   Ⓓ $bc - aci$

2. Which of these expressions is equal to $4 - 7i$?

   Ⓐ $(6 - i) - (2 - 8i)$

   Ⓑ $(6 + i) - (2 + 8i)$

   Ⓒ $(6 + i) + (2 + 8i)$

   Ⓓ $(6 - i) + (2 - 8i)$

Select all correct answers.

3. Circle each sum, difference, or product that can be simplified to $6 - 3i$.

$$(9 - 5i) + (3 - 2i)$$
$$(4 + 2i) + (2 - 5i)$$
$$(9 - 5i) - (3 - 2i)$$
$$(4 + 2i) - (2 - 5i)$$
$$3i(-1 + 2i)$$
$$3i(-1 - 2i)$$

Match each sum, difference, or product with its simplified form.

_____ 4. $(6 - i) + (6 - 2i)$ **A** 12

_____ 5. $(6 - 2i) + (6 + 2i)$ **B** 39

                                C 40

_____ 6. $(6 - i) - (6 - 2i)$ **D** i

_____ 7. $(6 - 2i) - (6 + 2i)$ **E** $-3i$

                                F $-4i$

_____ 8. $(6 - i)(6 - 2i)$ **G** $12 - 3i$

_____ 9. $(6 - 2i)(6 + 2i)$ **H** $34 - 18i$

CONSTRUCTED RESPONSE

10. Find $a + b$, $a - b$, and ab when $a = 1 - 4i$ and $b = 3 + 3i$.

    _____

    _____

    _____

11. State the property that justifies each step in simplifying the product $i(a + bi)$.

$i(a + bi) = ia + i(bi)$ _____

           $= ai + (bi)i$ _____

           $= ai + bi^2$ Associative prop. of mult. and definition of squaring

           $= ai + b(-1)$ _____

           $= b(-1) + ai$ _____

           $= -b + ai$ Mult. prop. of -1

12. Find real numbers a and b such that the product $(a + bi)(3 - 6i)$ simplifies to a real number. Then substitute those values of a and b into the given expression and simplify.

    _____

    _____

    _____

13. a. Find the product $(3 + 4i)(3 + 4i)$.

    _____

    b. Find the product $(3 + 4i)(3 - 4i)$.

    _____

    c. Using your results from parts a and b as a guide, write a general form for the products $(a + bi)(a + bi)$ and $(a + bi)(a - bi)$, where a and b are real numbers.

    _____

    _____

14. Complete the table of values. Describe the pattern you see. Then use the pattern to find the values of i^9, i^{26}, and i^{100}. Explain your reasoning.

i	i^2	i^3	i^4	i^5	i^6	i^7	i^8
$\sqrt{-1}$							

_____

_____

_____

_____

The student will solve quadratic equations with real coefficients that have complex solutions.

SELECTED RESPONSE

Select the correct answer.

1. Solve $x^2 + 3x + 4 = 0$ over the set of complex numbers.

   Ⓐ $x = -3 \pm i\sqrt{7}$

   Ⓑ $x = -\dfrac{3}{2} \pm \dfrac{\sqrt{7}}{2}i$

   Ⓒ $x = -\dfrac{3}{2} \pm \dfrac{\sqrt{7}}{2}$

   Ⓓ $x = -1$ or $x = 4$

2. Solve $x^2 + 2x + 5 = 0$ over the set of complex numbers.

   Ⓐ $x = 1$ or $x = -3$

   Ⓑ $x = -1 \pm 2i$

   Ⓒ $x = \pm 2i$

   Ⓓ $x = -2 \pm 4i$

Select all correct answers.

3. Which of the following are solutions of the equation $x^2 + 27 = 0$ over the set of complex numbers?

   Ⓐ $3\sqrt{3}$ Ⓓ $-3\sqrt{3}$

   Ⓑ $i\sqrt{3}$ Ⓔ $-i\sqrt{3}$

   Ⓒ $3i\sqrt{3}$ Ⓕ $-3i\sqrt{3}$

Match each equation with its solutions over the set of complex numbers.

Using the list of numbers at the right, write the solutions for each equation.

4. $x^2 + 4 = 0$ [_____]

5. $x^2 - 4 = 0$ [_____]

6. $x^2 + 4x + 12 = 0$ [_____]

7. $x^2 - 4x + 8 = 0$ [_____]

| ± 2 |
| $\pm 2i$ |
| $2 \pm 2i$ |
| $-2 \pm 2i$ |
| $2 \pm 2i\sqrt{2}$ |
| $-2 \pm 2i\sqrt{2}$ |

CONSTRUCTED RESPONSE

8. Describe the solutions of the equation $4x^2 + 6x + 3 = 0$ as real or non-real. Then solve the equation over the set of complex numbers.

   _____

   _____

9. Consider the equation $7x^2 - 2x + 9 = 2x^2 - 5x + 8$.

   a. Rewrite the equation in the form $ax^2 + bx + c = 0$.

   _____

   b. Describe the solution(s) of the equation as real or non-real.

   _____

   c. Solve the equation over the set of complex numbers.

   _____

   _____

10. Marco says that the solutions of the equation $x^2 + 6x + 13 = 0$ are $x = -1$ and $x = -5$. Is Marco correct? If so, verify his solutions by solving the equation for x over the set of complex numbers. If not, explain his error and provide the correct solutions.

    _____

    _____

    _____

    _____

11. Consider the equation $4x^2 + 8x + c = 0$.

   a. Describe all values of c such that the equation $4x^2 + 8x + c = 0$ has two non-real solutions. Explain.

_____

_____

_____

   b. Solve the equation $4x^2 + 8x + 13 = 0$ over the set of complex numbers.

_____

_____

12. Do the equations $x^2 - 4x + 21 = 0$ and $x^2 + 4x - 21 = 0$ have the same type (real or non-real) and number of solutions? Describe the solutions of each equation, and then solve each equation over the set of complex numbers.

_____

_____

_____

_____

The student will extend polynomial identities to the complex numbers.

SELECTED RESPONSE
Select the correct answer.

1. Factor $x^2 + 121$ over the set of complex numbers.

   Ⓐ $(x + 11)(x - 11)$

   Ⓑ $(x + 11i)(x + 11i)$

   Ⓒ $(x + 11i)(x - 11i)$

   Ⓓ $(x - 11i)(x - 11i)$

2. Factor $x^2 + 4x + 5$ over the set of complex numbers.

   Ⓐ $(x - 1)(x + 5)$

   Ⓑ $(x - (2 + i))(x - (2 - i))$

   Ⓒ $(x + (-2 + i))(x + (-2 - i))$

   Ⓓ $(x - (-2 + i))(x - (-2 - i))$

3. Factor $x^2 + 10ix - 25$ over the set of complex numbers.

   Ⓐ $(x - 5i)^2$

   Ⓑ $(x + 5i)^2$

   Ⓒ $(x - 5i)(x + 5i)$

   Ⓓ $(x - 5)(x + 5)$

Match each expression with its factorization over the set of complex numbers.

_____ 4. $25x^2 + 20ix - 4$ **A** $(5x + 2)(5x - 2)$

_____ 5. $25x^2 + 4$ **B** $(5x + 2i)(5x - 2i)$

                         C $(5x + 2)^2$

_____ 6. $25x^2 - 20x + 4$ **D** $(5x - 2)^2$

                         E $(5x - 2i)^2$

                         F $(5x + 2i)^2$

CONSTRUCTED RESPONSE

7. Factor the left side of the equation $4x^2 + 12ix - 9 = 0$ over the set of complex numbers. Then solve the equation.

   _____

   _____

   _____

8. Describe two different ways to solve the equation $9x^2 + 144 = 0$ over the set of complex numbers. Then solve the equation both ways, verifying that the solutions are the same.

   _____

   _____

   _____

   _____

   _____

   _____

   _____

9. Solve the equation $x^2 + 2x + 5 = 0$ using the quadratic formula. Then use the solutions to write the factorization of $x^2 + 2x + 5$ over the set of complex numbers.

   _____

   _____

   _____

10. Consider the expressions $(2x + 7)^2$ and $(2x + 7i)^2$.

   a. Write each expression in the form $ax^2 + bx + c$ where a, b, and c are complex numbers.

   _____

   _____

   b. Compare, term by term, the two results from part a. Explain any differences.

   _____

   _____

   c. Suppose you take the expression $(2x + 7i)^2$ and move the i from the constant to the coefficient of x to obtain the expression $(2ix + 7)^2$. Describe the effect this change will have on the expansion of the expression without actually expanding the expression.

   _____

   _____

   _____

   _____

11. Write a polynomial identity that can be used to factor $a^2 + b^2$. How does this polynomial identity compare to the identity $a^2 - b^2 = (a + b)(a - b)$? Use the appropriate identity to rewrite $144x^2 + 25y^2$ and $144x^2 - 25y^2$.

   _____

   _____

   _____

   _____

   _____

   _____

   _____

   _____

The student will know the Fundamental Theorem of Algebra and show that it is true for quadratic polynomials.

SELECTED RESPONSE

Select the correct answer.

1. How many roots does the polynomial $x^3 + 6x^2 + 12x + 8$ have in the set of complex numbers?

   (A) 0

   (B) 1

   (C) 2

   (D) 3

2. A certain equation of the form $ax^2 + bx + c = 0$, where a, b, and c are real numbers, has one real solution. How many non-real solutions does the equation have?

   (A) 0

   (B) 1

   (C) 2

   (D) 3

Select all correct answers.

3. Choose all polynomials that have two complex roots.

   (A) $x^2 + 4x + 18$

   (B) $x^3 + 5x^2 + 8x + 4$

   (C) $x^2 - 8x + 16$

   (D) $x^4 - 16$

   (E) $x^2 - 144$

   (F) $x^2 + 121$

Select the correct answer for each lettered part.

4. Use the corollary of the fundamental theorem of algebra to find the number of complex roots for each polynomial.

   a. $x^2 + 4x + 4$ ○ 1 ○ 2 ○ 3 ○ 4

   b. $12x^2 + 4x^3 + 2x + 1$ ○ 1 ○ 2 ○ 3 ○ 4

   c. $x^4 - 2x^2 + 2x$ ○ 1 ○ 2 ○ 3 ○ 4

   d. $x^3 - 81$ ○ 1 ○ 2 ○ 3 ○ 4

CONSTRUCTED RESPONSE

5. Use the fundamental theorem of algebra and its corollary to identify the number of complex roots that the polynomial $x^2 + 4x + 12$ has. Then find the roots.

   _____

   _____

   _____

   _____

6. Sheila says that $x^2 - 18x + 81$ has one real root, 9. She uses the corollary of the fundamental theorem of algebra to conclude that the polynomial must have one non-real root. Is Sheila correct? Explain. Then state all complex roots of the polynomial.

   _____

   _____

   _____

   _____

7. Consider the equation $(x^2 - 4)(x^2 + 4)(x^2 + 6x + 9) = 0$.

   a. How many complex solutions does the equation have? Explain.

   _____

   _____

   _____

   _____

   b. Find each complex solution, listing any repeated solution once for each occurrence.

   _____

   _____

8. A polynomial has complex roots a and b.

   a. If these are the only complex roots of the polynomial (neither root is repeated), what is the degree of the polynomial? How do you know?

   _____

   _____

   _____

   b. How does multiplying the polynomial by a nonzero constant c affect the degree of the polynomial? Describe the complex roots of the resulting polynomial.

   _____

   _____

   _____

   c. How does multiplying the polynomial by the binomial $x - c$ affect the degree of the polynomial? Describe the complex roots of the resulting polynomial.

   _____

   _____

   _____

9. Explain how the quadratic formula supports the corollary of the fundamental theorem of algebra.

   _____

   _____

   _____

   _____

   _____

   _____

   _____

   _____

   _____

   _____

The student will interpret parts of an expression, such as terms, factors, and coefficients.

SELECTED RESPONSE
Select the correct answer.

1. Elena, Brian, Carmen, and Drew carpool to work every weekday morning. The fuel efficiency of Brian's car is m miles per gallon driving on the highway and 4 miles per gallon less than that driving in the city. Their commute to work is 20 miles on the highway and 8 miles in the city. The total amount of gas consumed driving to work in Brian's car is given by the expression $\dfrac{20}{m} + \dfrac{8}{m-4}$. What is the meaning of the term $\dfrac{8}{m-4}$ in the context of the problem?

   (A) The amount of gas consumed driving on the highway

   (B) The total amount of gas consumed driving to work

   (C) The amount of gas consumed driving in the city

   (D) The number of miles driven in the city

2. A 9 in. by 18 in. sheet of cardboard is being made into a box for a class project. As shown below, squares with side length x are cut from each corner of the sheet, and then the sides are folded up to form the box. One expression for the volume of the box is $(18 - 2x)(9 - 2x)x$. Interpret the first factor, $18 - 2x$, in the context of the problem.

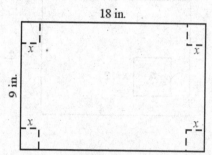

   (A) The factor $18 - 2x$ represents the height of the box.

   (B) The factor $18 - 2x$ represents the length of the box.

   (C) The factor $18 - 2x$ represents the width of the box.

   (D) The factor $18 - 2x$ represents the volume of the box.

Use the following information to match each verbal description with the corresponding mathematical expression.

A sculpture is made up of a solid pedestal with five solid spheres stacked on top. The pedestal has a length and width of $2x$ and a height of x. Three of the spheres have a radius of $x + 1$, while the other two spheres have a radius of $x - 4$.

The total volume of the sculpture is $4x^3 + 4\pi(x+1)^3 + \dfrac{8}{3}\pi(x-4)^3$.

_____ 3. The combined volume of the five spheres

_____ 4. The volume of just one of the larger spheres

_____ 5. The volume of the square pedestal

_____ 6. The combined volume of the smaller spheres

A $4x^3$

B $4x^2$

C $\dfrac{4}{3}\pi(x-4)^3$

D $\dfrac{4}{3}\pi(x+1)^3$

E $\dfrac{8}{3}\pi(x-4)^3$

F $4\pi(x+1)^3 + \dfrac{8}{3}\pi(x-4)^3$

Name _____ Date _____ Class_____

CONSTRUCTED RESPONSE

7. A coin is randomly tossed onto the rectangular mat shown. The probability that the coin lands in square region A is given by the expression $\dfrac{(x+2)^2}{(2x+5)(3x-2)}$.

Interpret the expressions $x+2$, $(x+2)^2$, and $(2x+5)(3x-2)$ in the context of the problem.

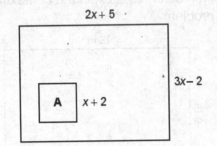

_____

_____

8. For a class project, Andre is making a cylinder with closed ends out of construction paper. An expression for the amount of construction paper needed is $2\pi r^2 + 2\pi rh$, where r is the cylinder's radius and h is the cylinder's height.

a. Interpret each term in the expression $2\pi r^2 + 2\pi rh$.

_____

_____

b. Both terms contain a factor of 2. Does this factor represent the same thing in each term? Explain.

_____

_____

c. Determine the surface area of Andre's cylinder if it has radius 3 in. and height 6 in.

_____

9. Sandra has just started a new job. At the end of each year, she will be given a 2.5% raise. An expression that models the total amount of money Sandra earns after n years on the job is $40,000\left(\dfrac{1-(1.025)^n}{1-1.025}\right)$. Interpret each quantity in the context of the problem.

a. 40,000

_____

b. 1.025

_____

c. $(1.025)^n$

_____

10. The volume of a rectangular box is given by the expression $x^3 + 3x^2 - 6x - 8$. The height of the box is $x - 2$, where x is an integer greater than 2. Find the quotient of $x^3 + 3x^2 - 6x - 8$ and $x - 2$. Interpret the result in the context of the problem.

_____

_____

_____

11. Janine and Adam are building the set for the school play. If each worked alone, Adam would take 3 days longer than Janine to build the set. Adam works for one day by himself, and then Janine helps him for five days. Write expressions that represent the fraction of the set each person has built so far. Interpret the numerator and denominator in each expression.

_____

_____

_____

Name _____ Date _____ Class_____

The student will interpret complicated expressions by viewing one or more of their parts as a single entity.

SELECTED RESPONSE
Select the correct answer.

1. The science club is planning a field trip to a museum. Each student will pay $10 for admission and an equal share of the $200 transportation cost. The cost function $C(s) = \dfrac{200}{s} + 10$ represents the total cost per student when s students go on the field trip. To what does the term $\dfrac{200}{s}$ in the cost function correspond?

   (A) Each student's cost for admission

   (B) Each student's share of the transportation cost

   (C) The number of students who go on the trip

   (D) The total cost per student

2. To frame a square piece of artwork such as a photo or print, a framing store bases its charge on the perimeter P, in inches, of the frame needed to surround both the artwork and a border around the artwork called a mat. A particular style of frame costs $1.50 per inch, while the glass costs $0.10 per square inch and the mat costs $0.15 per square inch. There is also a flat labor charge of $30. The total charge C for the framing is given by the function $C(P) = 1.5P + 0.25\left(\dfrac{P}{4}\right)^2 + 30$. In this function, what does the expression $0.25\left(\dfrac{P}{4}\right)^2$ represent?

   (A) The charge for the frame

   (B) The charge for the glass

   (C) The charge for the mat

   (D) The combined charge for the glass and mat

3. Consider a cube with edge length s. What does the expression $\dfrac{s^3}{6s^2}$ represent?

   (A) The ratio of the surface area of the cube to the volume of the cube

   (B) The ratio of the area of one face of the cube to the total surface area of the cube

   (C) The ratio of the volume of the cube to the surface area of the cube

   (D) The ratio of the total surface area of the cube to the area of one face of the cube

4. Joseph knows that he paddles his canoe at 6 miles per hour in still water. One day Joseph paddles 15 miles upstream (against the current) and then paddles back to his campsite. The 30 mile trip takes 9 hours to complete. Joseph uses the equation $9 = \dfrac{15}{6-c} + \dfrac{15}{6+c}$ to find c, the speed of the river's current. What does the expression $\dfrac{15}{6+c}$ represent?

   (A) The canoe's rate when Joseph paddles upstream

   (B) The canoe's rate when Joseph paddles downstream

   (C) The time it takes Joseph to paddle upstream

   (D) The time it takes Joseph to paddle downstream

CONSTRUCTED RESPONSE

5. The formula $A = s^2 + 4sh$ gives the surface area of a glass vase in the shape of a rectangular prism having height h and a square base with side length s. What are the meanings of the expressions s^2 and $4sh$ in the formula?

   _____

   _____

Name _____ Date _____ Class _____

6. A new sculpture in a public park consists of spheres, cubes, and cones made of solid concrete. The spheres and the base of the cones have radius r meters, the cubes have edge length s meters, and the cones have height s meters. The expression $12\pi r^3 + \pi r^2 s + 5s^3$ represents the volume of concrete, in cubic meters, used to make the sculpture.

a. Which term corresponds to the combined volume of the spheres?

_____

b. Which term corresponds to the combined volume of the cubes?

_____

c. Which term corresponds to the combined volume of the cones?

_____

d. How many spheres are in the sculpture?

_____

e. How many cubes are in the sculpture?

_____

f. How many cones are in the sculpture?

_____

7. A commercial airline allows the sum of the length, width, and height of carry-on luggage to be at most 45 inches. For a carry-on that has cross-sectional area A (equal to the product of the height and the width), the formula $V = A\left(45 - h - \dfrac{A}{h}\right)$ gives the volume of the luggage with maximum allowable dimensions. In the formula, h represents height. What do $\dfrac{A}{h}$ and $45 - h - \dfrac{A}{h}$ represent?

_____

8. A cylindrical can holds a fixed volume V. The function $A = 2\pi r^2 + \dfrac{2V}{r}$ gives the total surface area A of the can in terms of the radius r. What do the expressions $2\pi r^2$ and $\dfrac{2V}{r}$ represent in this function? Explain your reasoning.

_____

_____

_____

_____

9. Aisha and her dog Karl are at the beach. Aisha throws a tennis ball into the water for Karl to retrieve. Karl runs 10 feet per second and swims 3 feet per second. The expression $\dfrac{d}{10} + \dfrac{\sqrt{30^2 + (72-d)^2}}{3}$ represents the time Karl takes to get to the ball by running a distance d, in feet, along the beach and then swimming straight to the ball.

a. What is the meaning of each term in the expression? How is it derived?

_____

_____

_____

_____

_____

_____

b. How far did Aisha throw the ball? Explain your reasoning.

_____

_____

_____

_____

_____

The student will use the structure of an expression to identify ways to rewrite it.

SELECTED RESPONSE

Select the correct answer.

1. Circle the expression that makes a true statement.

   When $x^3 - 125$ is written as a product of a binomial and a trinomial, the trinomial factor is

   $$\boxed{\begin{array}{l} x^2 - 5x + 25 \\ x^2 + 5x + 25 \\ x^2 - 10x + 25 \\ x^2 + 10x + 25 \end{array}}$$

2. Which of the following is not present in the simplified form of $\dfrac{a^3 + 216}{a^2 - 36}$?

   Ⓐ The constant term 36 in the numerator

   Ⓑ The linear term a in the denominator

   Ⓒ The linear term a in the numerator

   Ⓓ The constant term −6 in the denominator

Select all correct answers.

3. Determine which of the following expressions are equivalent to 4^x.

   Ⓐ $2 \cdot 2^x$

   Ⓑ $64 \cdot 4^x$

   Ⓒ $\dfrac{4^{x+1}}{16}$

   Ⓓ $\left(2^x\right)^2$

   Ⓔ $\dfrac{4^{x+3}}{64}$

   Ⓕ $16^{\frac{1}{4}x}$

Match each expression with its equivalent factored form.

____ 4. $n^2 - 64$

____ 5. $n^2 + 16n + 64$

____ 6. $n^3 - 64$

____ 7. $n^3 + 64$

A $(n-4)\left(n^2 + 4n + 16\right)$

B $(n+4)^3$

C $(n+8)^2$

D $(n+4)\left(n^2 - 4n + 16\right)$

E $(n+4)(n-4)$

F $(n+8)(n-8)$

CONSTRUCTED RESPONSE

8. Write $x^6 - 729$ in factored form. Show your work.

_____

_____

_____

9. The present value of an investment of p_0 dollars at 7% interest, compounded annually, can be represented by $p_0 \cdot 1.07^t$, where t is the number of years since the investment was made. At any time t, the value of the investment 10 years later can be represented by $p_0 \cdot 1.07^{t+10}$. How does the value of the investment 10 years later compare with the present value at any time t?

_____

_____

_____

10. Bill attempted to factor $a^6 - b^6$ as shown below. His teactold her him that his factorization wasn't complete because the expression $a^4 + a^2b^2 + b^4$ can be factored further. What help can you give Bill to find a complete factorization?

$$a^6 - b^6 = \left(a^2\right)^3 - \left(b^2\right)^3$$
$$= \left(a^2 - b^2\right)\left(a^4 + a^2b^2 + b^4\right)$$
$$= (a+b)(a-b)\left(a^4 + a^2b^2 + b^4\right)$$

_____

_____

_____

_____

11. Justin is taking part in a run for charity. He has $250 in pledges just for running and $40 in pledges for every mile he runs. Write an expression that represents the total amount of money Justin raises for every mile m he runs as a single fraction, and then rewrite the expression as a sum of simplified fractions.

_____

_____

12. Luize buys table space in the artist's alley at a comic convention for $30 so she can sell her art prints. The paper and ink supplies cost her $2 per print. She decides to sell her prints for $3.50 each.

a. Write an expression for the profit Luize makes from selling p prints.

_____

b. Write an expression for the profit Luize makes per print from selling p prints. Write this expression as a single fraction.

_____

c. Rewrite the expression in part b as a sum or difference of two simplified fractions.

_____

d. Does Luize's profit per print increase or decrease as she sells more prints? Explain.

_____

_____

_____

The student will use the properties of exponents to transform expressions for exponential functions.

SELECTED RESPONSE

Select the correct answer.

1. Which of the following is equivalent to

   $f(x) = 27^{\frac{5}{3}x}$?

   Ⓐ $g(x) = 45^x$

   Ⓑ $g(x) = 15^x$

   Ⓒ $g(x) = 243^x$

   Ⓓ $g(x) = 125^x$

2. Which of the following cannot be rewritten in the form $f(x) = a^x$ where a is a rational number?

   Ⓐ $f(x) = 32^{\frac{4}{5}x}$

   Ⓑ $f(x) = 16^{\frac{2}{3}x}$

   Ⓒ $f(x) = \left(\frac{1}{81}\right)^{\frac{x}{4}}$

   Ⓓ $f(x) = 216^{\frac{2}{3}x}$

3. The population of a colony of bacteria doubles every 8 hours. If the number of bacteria starts at 80, the population P after t hours is given by $P(t) = 80 \cdot 2^{\frac{t}{8}}$. What is an equivalent form of $P(t)$ that shows the approximate hourly growth factor for the bacteria population?

   Ⓐ $P(t) = 80 \cdot 1.091^t$

   Ⓑ $P(t) = 80 \cdot 1.125^t$

   Ⓒ $P(t) = 80 \cdot 1.25^t$

   Ⓓ $P(t) = 80 \cdot 1.414^t$

Select all correct answers.

4. Circle each function that is equivalent to

   $f(x) = 8^{\frac{5}{3}x}$.

   $g(x) = 32 \cdot 256^{\frac{1}{3}x}$

   $g(x) = 64^{\frac{5}{6}x}$

   $g(x) = 128^{\frac{6}{7}x}$

   $g(x) = 4^{\frac{5}{2}x}$

   $g(x) = 16 \cdot 16^{\frac{3}{4}x}$

CONSTRUCTED RESPONSE

5. Rewrite $g(x) = 81^{\frac{7}{5}x}$ as an exponential function with base 27. Show your work.

   _____

   _____

   _____

6. A scientist has 64 milligrams of the radioactive isotope Fermium-253. The half-life of this isotope is about 3 days.

   a. Write a function in the form

      $f(t) = a\left(\frac{1}{2}\right)^{ct}$ for the amount f of

      Fermium-253 remaining after t days.

   _____

   b. Use the result from part a to write a function that is equivalent to $f(t)$ and that shows the percent (as a decimal) of the isotope remaining after each week. Explain your reasoning, show your work, and state what percent of the isotope remains after each week.

   _____

   _____

7. How many times greater is the value of $g(x) = 4^{\frac{3}{2}x}$ compared to the value of $f(x) = 4^x$ for any value of x? Explain your reasoning.

_____

_____

_____

8. An investment of $4600 earns 5% interest compounded annually. The value V of the investment after t years is given by the function $V(t) = 4600(1.05)^t$.

   a. Use properties of exponents to rewrite the given function as another function that shows the approximate quarterly interest rate of the investment. Explain your reasoning, and show your work. State what the approximate quarterly interest rate is.

   _____

   _____

   b. Use properties of exponents to rewrite the given function as another function that shows the approximate monthly interest rate of the investment. Explain your reasoning, and show your work. State what the approximate monthly interest rate is.

   _____

   _____

   c. Describe how you could use the function in part a to obtain the function in part b. Show that your method works. Is there any drawback to this method?

   _____

   _____

   _____

   d. How are the annual, quarterly, and monthly interest rates mathematically related?

   _____

   _____

9. For the period 1880–1970, an exponential regression model that gives the population P of Dallas, Texas, t decades after 1880 is $P(t) = 18,800(1.58)^t$. Transform the model to find the annual growth rate. Explain your reasoning, and show your work. By approximately what percent was the population of Dallas growing every 10 years? Every year?

_____

_____

_____

_____

The student will derive the formula for the sum of a finite geometric series, and use the formula to solve problems.

SELECTED RESPONSE
Select the correct answer.

1. A car decelerates such that each second it travels 5% less than the distance it traveled in the previous second. About how far does the car travel in 5 seconds if it is traveling at 30 meters per second during the first second of deceleration?

   Ⓐ 100.0 m

   Ⓑ 135.7 m

   Ⓒ 142.5 m

   Ⓓ 165.8 m

2. Sven earns $750 in his first month at a new part-time job. If his pay rate increases by 0.5% each month, how much will Sven have earned after one year?

   Ⓐ $796.26

   Ⓑ $9045.00

   Ⓒ $9251.67

   Ⓓ $11,937.84

Select all correct answers.

3. Artur decides to take up building model cars as a hobby. The first car he builds takes him 16 hours. Determine which of the following statements about Artur are true if each car he builds takes him 94% as long as the previous car.

   Ⓐ It will take Artur about 58.5 hours to build his first 4 cars.

   Ⓑ It will take Artur about 67.3 hours to build his first 5 cars.

   Ⓒ It will take Artur about 85.1 hours to build his first 6 cars.

   Ⓓ It will take Artur about 89.8 hours to build his first 7 cars.

   Ⓔ It will take Artur about 104.1 hours to build his first 8 cars.

4. For each amount and annual interest rate in the table, use the formula for the sum of a finite geometric series to determine whether depositing that amount of money into a bank account at the beginning of every year for four years will result in an account balance of at least $5000 at the time the fourth deposit is made. Assume that interest is compounded annually. Indicate your answer by putting a check mark in the appropriate column.

	Yes	No
$1000; 9% interest		
$1200; 5% interest		
$1150; 7% interest		
$1100; 7.5% interest		
$1050; 8.5% interest		

CONSTRUCTED RESPONSE

5. Given the finite geometric series $a + ar + ar^2 + ar^3 + \ldots + ar^{n-1}$ where $r \neq 1$, you can obtain a formula for the sum $S_n = a + ar + ar^2 + ar^3 + \ldots + ar^{n-1}$ by multiplying by the common ratio r to get $rS_n = ar + ar^2 + ar^3 + \ldots + ar^{n-1} + ar^n$. Describe and show the steps that you must take next to arrive at a formula for S_n.

   _____

   _____

   _____

6. You deposit $200 at the beginning of every year for four years into a savings account that pays 5% interest compounded annually. If you make no withdrawals or other deposits, how much money is in the account when you make your fourth deposit? Show your work.

   _____

   _____

   _____

7. A student in a physical education class bounces a ball hard against the gymnasium floor. The first bounce travels 20 feet into the air, while each successive bounce reaches three-quarters of the height of the previous bounce. Write a formula for the total vertical distance the ball travels after n bounces, and explain your reasoning. To the nearest foot, how far does the ball travel vertically after 10 bounces?

_____

_____

_____

8. In 2012, the NCAA Men's Division I Basketball March Madness was a 68 team, single-elimination tournament, which means that competitors were eliminated after one loss. In the first round, each of the eight teams with the lowest seeds played another such team in one game, with the four winners advancing to the second round. The second round had 32 games, and in each subsequent round the number of games was halved. Seven rounds were played before a champion was determined. Use the formula for the sum of a finite geometric series to determine how many games were played. Show your work.

_____

_____

9. Shauna wants to pay off her $25,000 college debt in 7 years. The annual interest rate on the debt is 6%, and interest is compounded monthly.

a. Shauna wants to determine how large her debt would be in 7 years if left untouched so she can devise a payment plan. Because she intends to repay the debt in full, she will leave out of her calculations any and all fees that would result from ignoring her debt. Determine how large Shauna's fee-free debt would be in 7 years.

_____

b. Shauna decides to base her monthly repayment plan on the value calculated in part a. What would her monthly payment be if she makes equal monthly payments?

_____

c. Explain why the value from part b is not the actual monthly payment needed to pay off Shauna's debt.

_____

d. Determine the actual monthly payment Shauna can make to pay off the debt in 7 years. Explain your reasoning, and show your work.

_____

_____

_____

_____

The student will understand closure of polynomials under operations and will add, subtract, and multiply polynomials.

SELECTED RESPONSE

Select the correct answer.

1. Which of the following best describes the product of $ax^2 + bx + c$ and $mx^2 + nx + p$, where x is a variable and a, b, c, m, n, and p are nonzero real numbers?

   Ⓐ A quadratic polynomial

   Ⓑ An exponential expression

   Ⓒ A third-degree polynomial

   Ⓓ A fourth-degree polynomial

2. What is the coefficient of the x-term when subtracting $2x^5 + 7x^4 - 3x^3 + 4x^2 - 5x + 6$ from $3x^5 + 4x^4 + x^3 - 3x^2 - 3x - 1$?

   Ⓐ 2   Ⓒ -7

   Ⓑ 1   Ⓓ -8

3. When $2x^5 + 3x^4 - x^3 + 4x^2 - 5x + 7$ is multiplied by $7x^4 - 2x^3 + 4x^2 - 3x + 1$, what is the term with the highest degree in the product?

   Ⓐ $2x^5$

   Ⓑ 7

   Ⓒ $14x^9$

   Ⓓ $14x^{20}$

Select all correct answers.

4. Simplify each expression as needed to determine which ones represent third-degree polynomials.

   Ⓐ $(3x + 2)(2x - 1)(x^2 + 2)$

   Ⓑ $(2x^4 + 5x^3 - 3x^2 + 2x - 9) +$
      $(7 + 3x - x^2 + x^3 - 2x^4)$

   Ⓒ $(2x + 3)(3x + 1)(x - 7)$

   Ⓓ $(x^2 + 2x - 1)(2x^2 - 3x + 5)$

   Ⓔ $(2x^5 + 6x^4 - x^3 + 3x^2 + x + 5) -$
      $(2x^5 + 6x^4 - 8x^3 + 2x^2 - 2x + 14)$

CONSTRUCTED RESPONSE

5. Find the product. Show your work.

   $(3x - 2)(2x^2 - 5x + 1)$

   _____

   _____

   _____

6. Find the sum. Show your work.

   $(5x^4 - x^3 + 2x + 1) + (2x^3 + 3x^2 - 4x - 7)$

   _____

   _____

   _____

7. The polynomials below approximate the number of students in a large high school who were members of clubs A and B between the years 1990 and 2000, where t is the number of years after 1990.

   $$M_A(t) = -0.006t^4 - 0.025t^3 + 1.25t^2 + 2.5t + 31$$

   $$M_B(t) = -0.003t^4 - 0.15t^3 + 2.25t^2 + 1.25t + 19$$

   a. Find the polynomial $M_A(t) - M_B(t)$.
      Show your work.

      _____

      _____

      _____

   b. What does the polynomial $M_A(t) - M_B(t)$ represent?

      _____

      _____

8. Rectangular prism A has edges with lengths $x + 5$, $x + 2$, and $x + 1$. Rectangular prism B has edges with lengths $x + 3$, $x + 3$, and $x + 2$.

   a. Write a polynomial in standard form for the volume of each rectangular prism.

   _____

   b. For $x \geq 0$, which rectangular prism has greater volume? How do you know?

   _____

   c. Determine a polynomial expression that represents the positive difference in the volumes of the rectangular prisms.

   _____

9. Recall that a set of numbers is closed under an operation if performing the operation on any two numbers from the set always results in another number from the set. (In the case of division, the number you're dividing by cannot be 0, because then the operation wouldn't be defined.)

   a. Complete the table by indicating whether each set of numbers is closed under the four basic operations of addition, subtraction, multiplication, and division.

Set	Closed under addition?	Closed under subtraction?	Closed under multiplication?	Closed under division?
Whole numbers	Yes			
Integers	Yes			
Rational numbers	Yes			
Real numbers	Yes			

   b. In each instance where you said that a set wasn't closed, give an example to illustrate.

   _____

   _____

   c. Consider the set of all polynomials of the form $a_n x^n + a_{n-1} x^{n-1} + \cdots + a_2 x^2 + a_1 x + a_0$ where the coefficients $a_n, a_{n-1}, \ldots, a_2, a_1,$ and a_0 are real numbers. (Note: This set includes constants, linear polynomials, quadratic polynomials, and so on.) Is this set closed under all four basic operations? For any operation for which the set of polynomials is not closed, give an example to illustrate.

   _____

   _____

   d. With respect to closure, the set of polynomials in part c is most like which set of numbers in part a?

   _____

The student will know and apply the Remainder Theorem.

SELECTED RESPONSE

Select the correct answer.

1. For $p(x) = 4x^3 - 28x + 24$, the value of $p(-3)$ is 0. Which of the following must therefore be true?

   Ⓐ -3 is a factor of
   $p(x) = 4x^3 - 28x + 24$.

   Ⓑ $-3x$ is a factor of
   $p(x) = 4x^3 - 28x + 24$.

   Ⓒ $x - 3$ is a factor of
   $p(x) = 4x^3 - 28x + 24$.

   Ⓓ $x + 3$ is a factor of
   $p(x) = 4x^3 - 28x + 24$.

2. Use the remainder theorem to find the remainder when the polynomial $p(x) = x^3 + 3x^2 - 5x - 7$ is divided by $x + 5$.

   Ⓐ -182 Ⓒ -7

   Ⓑ -32 Ⓓ 168

3. The quotient when the polynomial $p(x) = x^3 - 3x^2 - 16x - 12$ is divided by $x - 1$ is $x^2 - 2x - 18 - \dfrac{30}{x-1}$. Which of the following is not necessarily true?

   Ⓐ $p(1) \neq 0$

   Ⓑ -1 is not a zero of $p(x)$.

   Ⓒ $x - 1$ is not a factor of $p(x)$.

   Ⓓ Substituting 1 for x in $p(x)$ results in -30.

Select all correct answers.

4. Use the remainder theorem and the factor theorem to determine which of the following binomials are factors of $p(x) = x^3 - 8x^2 + 5x + 14$.

   Ⓐ $x + 1$ Ⓓ $x - 2$

   Ⓑ $x + 3$ Ⓔ $x - 6$

   Ⓒ $x + 9$ Ⓕ $x - 7$

5. Use the remainder theorem and the factor theorem to determine whether the given binomial is a factor of the given polynomial. Indicate your answer by putting a check mark in the appropriate column of the table.

	Yes	No
$x + 5$; $x^3 + 2x^2 - 24x$		
$x + 1$; $x^3 + 6x^2 - x - 6$		
$x - 1$; $x^4 - 4x^3 + 6x^2 - 4x + 1$		
$x - 2$; $x^4 + 11x^3 + 36x^2 + 16x - 64$		
$x + 3$; $x^4 + 3x^3 - 12x^2 - 20x + 48$		

CONSTRUCTED RESPONSE

6. Use the remainder theorem to find the remainder when the polynomial $p(x) = x^4 - 4x^3 - 11x^2 + 66x - 72$ is divided by $x - 4$. Then use polynomial long division to verify the remainder.

   _____

   _____

   _____

   _____

   _____

   _____

   _____

7. Use the remainder theorem and the factor theorem to show that $x - 5$ is a factor of $p(x) = x^3 - 7x^2 + 2x + 40$. Then factor $p(x)$ completely.

   _____

   _____

   _____

8. Tyrell was asked to use the remainder theorem and the factor theorem to find, if possible, the linear factors of the polynomial $p(x) = x^3 - 9x^2 + 26x - 24$. He began by writing the following.

$$p(4) = 4^3 - 9(4)^2 + 26(4) - 24$$
$$= 64 - 144 + 104 - 24$$
$$= 0$$

Since $p(4) = 0$, $x + 4$ is a factor of $p(x)$.

a. Explain and correct Tyrell's mistake.

_____

_____

_____

_____

b. Find, if possible, the three linear factors of $p(x)$. Show your work.

_____

_____

_____

_____

_____

_____

9. The graph of $p(x) = x^3 - 9x^2 + 24x - 36$ is shown.

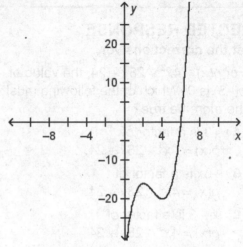

a. Examine the graph to identify a possible zero of the function $p(x)$. Then use substitution to show that it is a zero.

_____

_____

_____

b. Use the zero to write the function as the product of a linear factor and a quadratic factor.

_____

_____

_____

c. Algebraically confirm that the zero is not a repeated zero.

_____

_____

d. Explain why the function cannot be factored further over the set of real numbers.

_____

_____

The student will find zeros of polynomials using suitable factorizations, and use the zeros to draw the graph.

SELECTED RESPONSE
Select the correct answer.

1. Which of the following polynomial functions could have the graph shown?

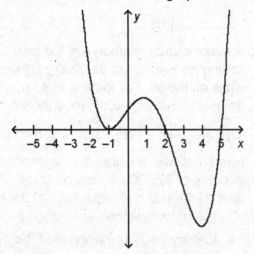

   Ⓐ $p(x) = (x - 1)(x + 2)(x + 5)$

   Ⓑ $p(x) = (x - 1)^2(x + 2)(x + 5)$

   Ⓒ $p(x) = (x + 1)(x - 2)(x - 5)$

   Ⓓ $p(x) = (x + 1)^2(x - 2)(x - 5)$

2. Which of the following is a true statement about the graph of the polynomial function $p(x) = (x - 4)(x + 2)(3x^2 + 6x)$?

   Ⓐ The graph crosses the x-axis four times and is never tangent to the x-axis.

   Ⓑ The graph crosses the x-axis three times and is never tangent to the x-axis.

   Ⓒ The graph crosses the x-axis two times and is tangent to the x-axis once.

   Ⓓ The graph crosses the x-axis three times and is tangent to the x-axis once.

Select all correct answers.

3. Which of the following are true statements about the graph of $p(x) = (x^2 - 8x + 16)(x^2 + 6x + 5)$?

   Ⓐ The graph crosses the x-axis at $x = -5$.

   Ⓑ The graph crosses the x-axis at $x = -1$.

   Ⓒ The graph crosses the x-axis at $x = 4$.

   Ⓓ The graph is tangent to the x-axis at $x = -5$.

   Ⓔ The graph is tangent to the x-axis at $x = -1$.

   Ⓕ The graph is tangent to the x-axis at $x = 4$.

4. Use the zeros of each polynomial function to determine whether its graph is ever tangent to the x-axis. Indicate your answer by putting a check mark in the appropriate column of the table.

	Yes	No
$p(x) = -(x - 3)(x + 5)^2$		
$p(x) = -(x^2 + 7x + 6)(x^2 - 2x - 8)$		
$p(x) = (x^2 - 6x + 9)(x^2 + 4x + 4)$		
$p(x) = 2x^3 + 6x^2 - 2x - 6$		
$p(x) = x^3 - 6x^2 + 12x - 8$		

CONSTRUCTED RESPONSE

5. Let $p(x) = -(x-3)^2(x^2 + 2x)$.

   a. Identify the zeros of the function. List all zeros as many times as they occur.

   _____

   _____

   _____

   b. Sketch a graph of the function.

   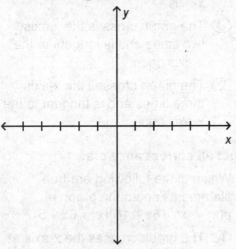

6. Let $p(x) = x^3 - 2x^2 - 4x + 8$.

   a. Identify the zeros of the function. List all zeros as many times as they occur.

   _____

   _____

   _____

   b. Sketch a graph of the function.

   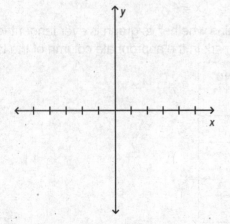

7. Suppose you are given a complete list of zeros of an unknown polynomial function. Can you sketch a graph of the function? If so, explain how. If not, explain why not and tell what additional information you would need in order to sketch the graph.

   _____

   _____

8. A major charity telethon has the goal of raising an average of $25,000 per hour while on the air. For the first eight hours the telethon is on the air, the function

   $D(t) = -\dfrac{1}{12}\left(t^3 - 12t^2 + 39t - 28\right)$ models

   how far above or below the target hourly average of $25,000 donations D are at time t, where D is in thousands of dollars and t is in hours since the telethon began.

   a. Identify the hours when the telethon is exactly at the target average at the end of those hours.

   _____

   _____

   b. Sketch a graph of the function.

   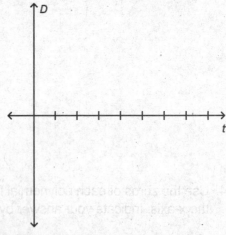

   c. Suppose the telethon met its target at the end of the tenth hour and exceeded it after that. Describe how the model and its graph would change.

   _____

   _____

The student will prove polynomial identities and use them to describe numerical relationships.

SELECTED RESPONSE
Select the correct answer.

1. Use the polynomial identity

   $$\left(x^2 - y^2\right)^2 + \left(2xy\right)^2 = \left(x^2 + y^2\right)^2$$

   with $x = 4$ and $y = 1$ to generate a Pythagorean triple.

   (A) $a = -15$, $b = 8$, and $c = 17$

   (B) $a = 225$, $b = 64$, and $c = 289$

   (C) $a = 15$, $b = 8$, and $c = 17$

   (D) $a = 3$, $b = 8$, and $c = 5$

2. You can use the polynomial identity $(a - b)^3 = a^3 - 3a^2b + 3ab^2 - b^3$ to determine the coefficients of the terms in the expanded form of a binomial raised to the third power without cubing the binomial. What is the coefficient of the x-term in the expanded form of $(2x - 5)^3$?

   (A) -125 (C) 8

   (B) -60 (D) 150

3. Circle the expression that makes a true statement.

   If you use the polynomial identity $(a + b)(a - b) = a^2 - b^2$ and mental math to calculate $35 \cdot 25$, the subtraction

   expression that results is
$1000 - 125$
$900 - 25$
$1050 - 175$
$1225 - 625$

CONSTRUCTED RESPONSE

4. Verify the polynomial identity $(a + b)(a - b) = a^2 - b^2$, and then use the identity and mental math to calculate $53 \cdot 47$. Show your work.

   _____

   _____

   _____

   _____

5. Verify the polynomial identity $(a + b)^3 = a^3 + 3a^2b + 3ab^2 + b^3$. Then use the identity to write $(3x + 2)^3$ in expanded form. Show your work.

   _____

   _____

   _____

   _____

   _____

   _____

6. Using the fact that a two-digit number with the digit a in the tens place and the digit b in the ones place can be written as $10a + b$, derive a polynomial identity for squaring a two-digit number. Then use your identity to find 57^2. Show your work.

   _____

   _____

   _____

   _____

   _____

   _____

7. Use the polynomial identities $(a + b)^3 = a^3 + 3a^2b + 3ab^2 + b^3$ and $(a - b)^3 = a^3 - 3a^2b + 3ab^2 - b^3$ to find 31^3 and 29^3. Show your work.

   _____

   _____

   _____

   _____

   _____

8. Mirelle operates a mail-order business from her home. She has two sizes of containers shaped like cubes. One has a side length of 42 cm, and the other has a side length of 38 cm. Mirelle wants to know the difference in the volumes of the two containers.

   a. Use the polynomial identity $(a + b)^3 = a^3 + 3a^2b + 3ab^2 + b^3$ to derive an identity for $(a - b)^3$. Show your work.

   _____

   _____

   _____

   _____

   _____

   b. Use the polynomial identities from part a to derive an identity for $(a + b)^3 - (a - b)^3$. Show your work.

   _____

   _____

   _____

   _____

   c. Use the identity from part b to find the difference in the volumes of the containers. Show your work.

   _____

   _____

   _____

   _____

9. The polynomial identity $(2m)^2 + (m^2 - 1)^2 = (m^2 + 1)^2$ can be used to generate a Pythagorean triple when m is an integer greater than 1.

   a. Verify the identity.

   _____

   _____

   _____

   _____

   _____

   b. A Pythagorean triple is called *primitive* when the numbers in the triple have no common factor other than 1. After experimenting with values of m, make a conjecture about when the identity generates primitive Pythagorean triples.

   _____

   _____

   _____

   _____

   c. Explain why primitive Pythagorean triples are not possible when m is odd.

   _____

   _____

   _____

   _____

Name _____ Date _____ Class_____

The student will know and apply the Binomial Theorem.

SELECTED RESPONSE

Select the correct answer.

1. What is the coefficient of the x^4-term in the expanded form of $(2x - 7)^6$?

   Ⓐ −11,760

   Ⓑ −784

   Ⓒ 784

   Ⓓ 11,760

2. Which variable term in the expanded form of $(3x + 1)^4$ has the greatest coefficient?

   Ⓐ The x-term

   Ⓑ The x^2-term

   Ⓒ The x^3-term

   Ⓓ The x^4-term

3. How many terms does the expanded form of $(2x^2 + 5)^9$ have?

   Ⓐ 8

   Ⓑ 9

   Ⓒ 10

   Ⓓ 11

Match each variable expression with the appropriate coefficient to produce the terms of the expanded form of $(2m + 3n)^5$.

____ 4. m^5 A 32

____ 5. m^4n B 240

____ 6. m^3n^2 C 243

____ 7. m^2n^3 D 720

____ 8. mn^4 E 810

____ 9. n^5 F 1080

CONSTRUCTED RESPONSE

10. Use the binomial theorem to write a polynomial identity for $(a - b)^5$. Show your work.

    _____

    _____

    _____

    _____

    _____

11. Without expanding the power, what is the x^5y^2-term in the expanded form of $(x - 2y)^7$? Show your work.

    _____

    _____

    _____

12. Use the binomial theorem to expand $(3x^2 + 2)^3$. Show your work.

    _____

    _____

    _____

    _____

13. The graph of the polynomial function $f(x) = 2x^3 - x^2 + 3x - 4$ passes through the point $(1, 0)$. Suppose you want to shift the graph 1 unit to the left so that the graph passes through the origin. This is the graph of a new function $g(x)$. Use the binomial theorem to find a rule for $g(x)$. Show your work.

    _____

    _____

    _____

    _____

14. Use the binomial theorem to expand $(x^2 + x - 1)^3$ and simplify the result. Show your work.

_____

_____

_____

_____

_____

The student will rewrite rational expressions in different forms using inspection, long division, or a computer.

SELECTED RESPONSE

Select the correct answer.

1. What is the result if you divide to rewrite the expression $\dfrac{3x^2 - x + 7}{x - 1}$?

    (A) $3x + \dfrac{2x + 7}{x - 1}$

    (B) $3x + 11$

    (C) $3x + 2$

    (D) $3x + 2 + \dfrac{9}{x - 1}$

2. When you divide to simplify the expression $\dfrac{6x^3 + 5x^2 + 2x + 7}{2x + 3}$, what is the fractional part of the quotient?

    (A) -5

    (B) $-\dfrac{5}{2x + 3}$

    (C) $\dfrac{7}{2x + 3}$

    (D) $3x^2 - 2x + 4$

Select all correct answers.

3. Circle each expression that is equivalent to $\dfrac{6x^2 + x - 2}{2x^2 + 5x - 3}$.

    $\dfrac{3x + 2}{x + 3}$

    $3 + \dfrac{1}{5} + \dfrac{2}{3}$

    $\dfrac{(2x - 1)(3x + 2)}{(x + 3)(2x - 1)}$

    $3 - \dfrac{7}{x + 3}$

    $\dfrac{3x}{x + 3} + \dfrac{2}{x + 3}$

    $\dfrac{3x - 2}{x - 3}$

CONSTRUCTED RESPONSE

4. Show that $\dfrac{6x^4 + 17x^3 + 18x^2 + 13x + 6}{2x^2 + 5x + 3}$ in simplified form is a polynomial.

    _____

    _____

    _____

    _____

    _____

    _____

5. The volume of a rectangular prism is $x^3 + 10x^2 + 31x + 30$ cubic centimeters. If the length is $x + 5$ centimeters and the width is $x + 2$ centimeters, determine a binomial expression for the height of the rectangular solid. Show your work.

    _____

    _____

    _____

    _____

    _____

    _____

6. Rewrite $\dfrac{x^4 + 2x^3 + x^2 + 8x - 9}{x^2 + 4}$ as the sum of a polynomial and a rational expression whose numerator is a constant. Show your work.

    _____

    _____

    _____

    _____

    _____

Name _____ Date _____ Class_____

7. The volume of a given sphere is $\frac{256}{3}\pi x^3 - 192\pi x^2 + 144\pi x - 36\pi$ cubic feet. The area of the circle formed by the intersection of a plane that passes through the center of the sphere is $16\pi x^2 - 24\pi x + 9\pi$ square feet. Complete the following parts to find the radius of the sphere. Show your work for each part. ·

a. Knowing that the formula for the volume V of a sphere with radius r is $V = \frac{4}{3}\pi r^3$, find r^3 in terms of x.

_____

_____

b. Knowing that the formula for the area A of a circle with radius r is $A = \pi r^2$, find r^2 in terms of x.

_____

_____

c. Divide the expression for r^3 by the expression for r^2 to find r.

_____

_____

_____

_____

_____

_____

8. If $\dfrac{2x^2 + 11x - 23}{x+7} = 2x + a - \dfrac{2}{x+7}$, what is the value of a? Show your work.

_____

_____

_____

_____

_____

_____

_____

_____

9. If $\dfrac{x^3 - x^2 + ax + b}{x^2 + 3x - 2}$ can be written as $x - 4 + \dfrac{2x+1}{x^2 + 3x - 2}$, what are the values of a and b? Show your work.

_____

_____

_____

_____

_____

_____

_____

The student will understand closure of rational expressions under operations and will perform operations on rational expressions.

SELECTED RESPONSE

Select the correct answer.

1. When $\dfrac{2x+4}{x+1}+\dfrac{5}{x-2}$ is written as a single rational expression, what is the numerator?

   (A) $2x+9$ (C) $2x^2+5x-7$

   (B) $2x-3$ (D) $2x^2+5x-3$

2. Which of the following simplify as a quotient of two binomials when the indicated operation is performed?

   (A) $\dfrac{x^2+4x}{x^2+2x-8}+\dfrac{3}{x-2}$

   (B) $\dfrac{x^2+x}{x^2+2x-15}-\dfrac{3}{x-3}$

   (C) $\dfrac{x^2+11x+30}{x^2+10x+21}\cdot\dfrac{x+3}{x+6}$

   (D) $\dfrac{x^2-10x+25}{x^2+3x-28}\div\dfrac{x-4}{x+7}$

   (E) $\dfrac{x^2-2x-24}{x^2+4x-5}\cdot\dfrac{x^2+3x-10}{x^2+x-12}\cdot$ $\dfrac{x^2-4x+3}{x^2-8x+12}$

Select the correct answer for each lettered part.

3. For the rational expressions $p(x)=\dfrac{x}{x+1}$ and $q(x)=\dfrac{1}{x+1}$, determine whether the result of performing each of the following operations is another rational expression.

   a. $p(x)+q(x)$ ○ Yes   ○ No

   b. $p(x)-q(x)$ ○ Yes   ○ No

   c. $p(x)\cdot q(x)$ ○ Yes   ○ No

   d. $\dfrac{p(x)}{q(x)}$ ○ Yes   ○ No

   e. $\dfrac{q(x)}{p(x)}$ ○ Yes   ○ No

CONSTRUCTED RESPONSE

4. Perform the division and simplify the result of $\dfrac{x^2+x-6}{x^2-6x-7}\div\dfrac{x^2-9x+14}{x^2+4x+3}$. Show your work. Identify all excluded values of x.

   _____

   _____

   _____

   _____

5. Perform the subtraction and simplify the result of $\dfrac{x^2-19}{x^2-x-56}-\dfrac{3}{x-8}$. Show your work. Identify all excluded values of x.

   _____

   _____

   _____

   _____

6. Let $p(x)$, $q(x)$, $r(x)$, and $s(x)$ be polynomials with $q(x)$, $r(x)$, and $s(x) \neq 0$. Use the rational expressions $\dfrac{p(x)}{q(x)}$ and $\dfrac{r(x)}{s(x)}$ along with the fact that the set of polynomials is closed under addition, subtraction, and multiplication to show that, like the set of rational numbers, the set of rational expressions is closed under the four basic operations.

   _____

   _____

   _____

   _____

   _____

7. Shamik lives 60 miles from a friend. Of those 60 miles, 50 are on the highway, and the rest are in a town where the speed limit is 20 miles per hour less than the highway speed limit.

   a. Write expressions for Shamik's highway travel time and town travel time in terms of his highway speed s when he visits his friend. Assume Shamik drives the appropriate speed limit for the entire trip.

   _____

   b. Determine Shamik's total travel time. Write the time as a single rational expression. Show your work.

   _____

   _____

   c. Determine Shamik's average travel speed. Show your work.

   _____

   _____

8. Claire was asked to evaluate $\dfrac{x^2+8x-33}{x^2-3x-54} \div \dfrac{x^2+17x+66}{x^2-12x+27}$ when $x=0$, $x=-2$, and $x=4$.

   To avoid having to evaluate four quadratic polynomials multiple times, Claire decided to simplify the expression before evaluating it for the first value of x. Her work is shown below.

   $$\dfrac{x^2+8x-33}{x^2-3x-54} \div \dfrac{x^2+17x+66}{x^2-12x+27} = \dfrac{(x+11)(x-3)}{(x+6)(x-9)} \div \dfrac{(x+6)(x+11)}{(x-3)(x-9)}$$
   $$= \dfrac{(x+6)(x-9)}{(x+11)(x-3)} \cdot \dfrac{(x+6)(x+11)}{(x-3)(x-9)}$$
   $$= \dfrac{(x+6)^2}{(x-3)^2}$$

   Now substitute 0 for x in the simplified expression $\dfrac{(x+6)^2}{(x-3)^2}$.

   $$\dfrac{(0+6)^2}{(0-3)^2} = \dfrac{6^2}{(-3)^2} = \dfrac{36}{9} = 4$$

   a. Explain how you can tell that Claire made a mistake by evaluating the original expression when $x=0$.

   _____

   b. Describe Claire's mistake.

   _____

   c. Simplify the expression correctly. Show your work.

   _____

   _____

   _____

Name _____ Date _____ Class_____

The student will create equations and inequalities in one variable and use them to solve problems.

SELECTED RESPONSE
Select the correct answer.

1. Circle the length that makes a true statement.

   The side length of a square is the positive square root of the side length of a larger square. If the difference in the areas of the two squares is 72 cm², the side length of the larger square is

3 cm
6 cm
9 cm
12 cm

2. To make an open rectangular box from an 8 inch by 12 inch sheet of cardboard, you cut squares with a side length of x inches from each corner of the sheet as shown and then fold up the sides to form the box. To determine the values of x that result in a volume of at least 60 in³, what inequality do you need to solve?

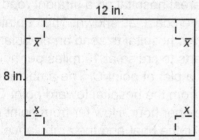

   (A) $x^3 - 10x^2 + 24x \leq 15$

   (B) $x^3 - 10x^2 + 24x \geq 15$

   (C) $x^3 - 20x^2 + 96x \geq 60$

   (D) $x^3 - 20x^2 + 96x \leq 60$

3. Raising 16 to a power that is 3 times some number is the same as raising 32 to twice the sum of the number and 2. What equation represents this?

   (A) $16^{3x} = 32^{2x+2}$

   (B) $16^{3+x} = 32^{2(x+2)}$

   (C) $16^{3+x} = 32^{2x+2}$

   (D) $16^{3x} = 32^{2(x+2)}$

4. Paolo can mow the lawn at his family's home in 2 hours. His younger sister Roberta needs 3 hours to mow the lawn. Paolo and Roberta would like to have 2 lawnmowers so they both can mow at the same time. The siblings need to know how much time working together would save to help convince their parents to get another lawnmower. What equation can the siblings use to determine the time t, in hours, needed to mow the lawn when they work together?

   (A) $\dfrac{t}{2} + \dfrac{t}{3} = 1$ (C) $\dfrac{t}{2} + \dfrac{t}{3} = \dfrac{1}{2}$

   (B) $2t + 3t = 1$ (D) $2t + 3t = \dfrac{1}{2}$

Select all correct answers.

5. The side length of a square is the positive square root of the side length of a larger square. The difference in the side lengths of the two squares is a positive number a and the difference in the areas of the squares is a positive number b. What equations can you use to determine the side lengths of the squares?

   (A) Let s represent the side length of the larger square, and solve $s - \sqrt{s} = a$.

   (B) Let s represent the side length of the smaller square, and solve $s - \sqrt{s} = a$.

   (C) Let s represent the side length of the larger square, and solve $s^2 - s = a$.

   (D) Let s represent the side length of the smaller square, and solve $s^2 - s = a$.

   (E) Let s represent the side length of the larger square, and solve $2as - a^2 = b$.

   (F) Let s represent the side length of the smaller square, and solve $2as - a^2 = b$.

   (G) Let s represent the side length of the larger square, and solve $2as + a^2 = b$.

   (H) Let s represent the side length of the smaller square, and solve $2as + a^2 = b$.

CONSTRUCTED RESPONSE

6. An air tanker is fighting a forest fire in a mountainous region. The tanker skims a lake to fill, flies with the wind to the fire, empties, and returns against the wind to the lake to refill. If the plane flies at 294 miles per hour in still air, the wind speed is 14 miles per hour, and one round trip from the lake to the fire and back takes at most 90 minutes, how far, at most, is the fire from the lake? Show your work.

_____

_____

_____

7. A red balloon and a blue balloon each contain 1 cubic unit of air. The red balloon begins to inflate, and its volume doubles each second. After the red balloon has been inflating for 7 seconds, the blue balloon begins to inflate, and its volume quadruples each second. After how many seconds are the volumes of the two balloons equal? Show your work.

_____

_____

_____

8. A freight train takes $4\frac{1}{2}$ hours longer to make a 420-mile trip than a passenger train. If the passenger train averages 30 miles per hour faster than the freight train, how long does it take the passenger train to make the trip? Show your work.

_____

_____

_____

9. A gardener wants to make a rectangular enclosure using a wall as one side and 160 m of fencing for the other three sides, as shown. For what values of x is the area of the enclosure more than 3000 m^2 but less than 3150 m^2? Show your work.

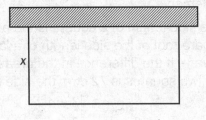

_____

_____

_____

_____

10. A crew member on a fishing boat needs medical attention. The boat is at point A, located 10 miles from point B, the nearest point on shore. Point B is 70 miles from the nearest hospital on a straight road along the coast, as shown. The captain radios the hospital to send an ambulance and starts to cruise at 15 miles per hour toward a pier at point C. The ambulance heads from the hospital toward point C at 75 miles per hour. How far from point B is point C if the boat and the ambulance arrive at the same time? Show your work.

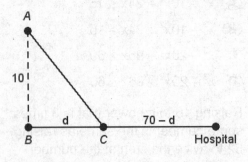

_____

_____

The student will create equations for relationships between quantities and graph equations on coordinate axes.

SELECTED RESPONSE

Select the correct answer.

1. A radioactive isotope has a half-life of 8 days. Which equation represents the time t, in days, it takes until p percent of the initial amount of the isotope remains?

   Ⓐ $p = 8\left(\dfrac{1}{2}\right)^{\frac{t}{100}}$

   Ⓑ $p = 100\left(\dfrac{1}{2}\right)^{\frac{t}{8}}$

   Ⓒ $p = 100(8)^{2t}$

   Ⓓ $p = \dfrac{1}{2}(8)^{\frac{t}{100}}$

2. The right triangle shown has base b, height h, an acute angle θ, and area A. Which of the following equations gives A in terms of b and θ?

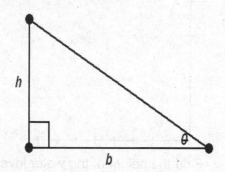

   Ⓐ $A = \dfrac{b^2 \tan\theta}{2}$

   Ⓑ $A = \dfrac{b^2 \cos\theta}{2}$

   Ⓒ $A = \dfrac{b^2 \sin\theta}{2}$

   Ⓓ $A = 2b^2 \tan\theta$

CONSTRUCTED RESPONSE

3. A soup company wants to make a new soup can that has a volume of 450 mL. Write an equation that relates the can's height h to the given volume and the radius r of the can, where h and r are measured in centimeters (remember that 1 mL = 1 cc^3). Then graph this relationship with the appropriate axis labels and scales.

   _____

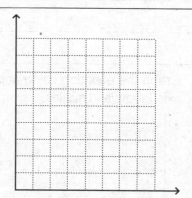

4. A rectangular piece of cardboard with perimeter 40 feet has three parallel creases, as shown. The cardboard is then folded to make a rectangular box with open rectangular ends. Write an equation that gives the volume V of the box, in cubic feet, in terms of x and y. Explain your reasoning.

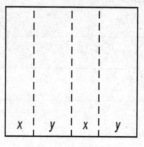

   _____
   _____
   _____

5. For an observer close to Earth's surface, an approximate model for the distance to the horizon is that the horizon distance varies directly as the square root of the height above the ground. For a height h of 1014 feet, the horizon distance d on a clear day is about 39 miles.

   a. Write an equation that relates horizon distance to the height above the ground for the given values. Show your work.

   _____

   _____

   _____

   _____

   b. Graph the equation using appropriate axis labels and scales.

   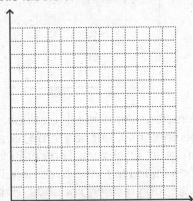

   c. Does doubling the height above the ground double the horizon distance? Explain.

   _____

   _____

   _____

6. High tide at a harbor occurred at noon one day. The water level at the end of a pier during high tide was 8.4 feet, and the water level at the end of the same pier during low tide 6 hours later was 0.2 feet. Assume that the next high tide is exactly 12 hours after the one at noon and that the weather conditions remain the same.

   a. Write an equation for the height h, in feet, of the water level at the end of the pier at time t, in hours after the high tide at noon. Explain your reasoning.

   _____

   _____

   _____

   b. Graph the equation using appropriate axis labels and scales.

   c. Find the height of the water level at the end of the pier at 3 a.m. the next day. Explain your reasoning.

   _____

   _____

   _____

The student will represent constraints by equations, inequalities, or systems, and interpret solutions in context.

SELECTED RESPONSE

Select the correct answer.

1. A farmer has 160 meters of fencing to make two enclosures, one for his goats and one for his pigs. The farmer plans to make a circular enclosure for his goats and a rectangular enclosure for his pigs. He plans to use between 20 meters and 30 meters of the fencing to make the pig enclosure. Based on these constraints, which describes the possibilities for the area A of the goat enclosure? Round to the nearest whole number as needed.

   Ⓐ $21 \text{ m}^2 \le A \le 22 \text{ m}^2$

   Ⓑ $1345 \text{ m}^2 \le A \le 1560 \text{ m}^2$

   Ⓒ $130 \text{ m}^2 \le A \le 140 \text{ m}^2$

   Ⓓ $5380 \text{ m}^2 \le A \le 6240 \text{ m}^2$

2. A beverage company is designing a cylindrical can for which the height is triple the radius. If the company wants the can to be between 300 and 400 cubic centimeters in volume, which of the following radius values satisfies this constraint? (Use 3.14 for π.)

   Ⓐ 2.5 cm   Ⓒ 3.75 cm

   Ⓑ 3.25 cm   Ⓓ 4.5 cm

Select all correct answers.

3. Sal plans to sell his old DVDs and CDs. Combined, he has 75 DVDs and CDs. He prices them at $1.50 per CD and $4.50 per DVD. Let d represent the number of DVDs Sal sells and let c represent the number of CDs he sells. He sells all of his DVDs and CDs and earns $262.50. Which of the following equations should be included in a system that reflects the constraints of this situation?

   Ⓐ $1.5c + 4.5d = 75$

   Ⓑ $c + d = 75$

   Ⓒ $1.5c = 262.50$

   Ⓓ $4.5d = 262.50$

   Ⓔ $1.5c + 4.5d = 262.50$

CONSTRUCTED RESPONSE

4. Bert will cut squares from the corners of a piece of cardboard as shown so he can fold up the resulting flaps to make a box.

   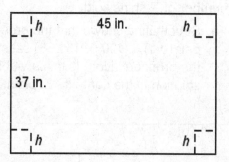

   Bert examines the volume function $V(h)$, where h is the box's height. He will solve for h under different constraints on the volume. What is the domain of the function $V(h)$ for values of h that are viable solutions in this context? Explain.

   _____

   _____

5. Amber owns 200 acres of farm land, and she wants to use it to grow corn and wheat. It takes 1.5 labor hours to produce (plant, grow, and harvest) an acre of corn and 1 labor hour to produce an acre of wheat. Her profit per acre of corn is $60, and her profit per acre of wheat is $45. Given that Amber has 300 labor hours at her disposal, determine four constraints she must consider when maximizing her profit function $P = 60c + 45w$, where c and w are the produced acres of corn and produced acres of wheat. Give each constraint algebraically, and explain.

   _____

   _____

   _____

   _____

6. The school art club is selling T-shirts and calendars to raise $750 to pay for an educational field trip. The art club makes a profit of $3.25 for each calendar sale and a profit of $2.50 for each T-shirt sale. An equation representing this situation is $3.25c + 2.50t = 750$, where c is the number of calendars sold and t is the number of T-shirts sold.

a. Substituting shows that the ordered pair $(c, t) = (100.5, 169.35)$ satisfies the profit equation. Is this a viable solution in the context? Explain.

_____

_____

b. You can rewrite the profit equation as $c = \dfrac{10(300 - t)}{13}$. Are there any viable solutions (c, t)? If so, give an example. If not, explain why not. (Hint: Think about what must be true about the factor $300 - t$ for c to be a whole number.)

_____

_____

c. Is an equation the best way to find viable, real-world solutions in this situation? Explain.

_____

_____

7. A juice company sells two kinds of juice blends in 1-gallon bottles. The regular mix uses $\dfrac{1}{2}$ gallon each of orange juice and pineapple juice, while the tropical mix combines $\dfrac{3}{4}$ gallon of orange juice with $\dfrac{1}{4}$ gallon of pineapple juice. Currently, the company has 225 gallons of orange juice and 150 gallons of pineapple juice on hand, and wants to maximize its profit from selling r bottles of the regular juice mix and t bottles of the tropical juice mix made using the juice on hand.

a. Give four constraints the company must take into consideration to maximize the profit.

_____

_____

_____

_____

b. Graph and shade the region that represents the constraints.

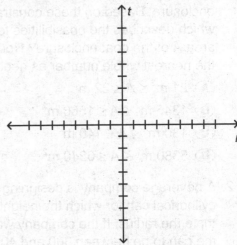

c. If the regular juice blend makes a profit of $2.50 per bottle sold and the tropical blend makes a profit of $1.75 per bottle sold, the profit from selling r bottles of regular blend and t bottles of tropical blend is $P = 2.5r + 1.75t$. The maximum profit is the maximum value found by evaluating the profit function at each vertex on the graph (or at the point in the shaded region that is closest to the vertex and has coordinates that make sense in the context). What is the maximum profit, and how many bottles of each type of juice blend will be sold to make that profit? Assume all bottles are sold.

_____

_____

_____

_____

The student will rearrange formulas to highlight a given quantity, using the same reasoning as in solving equations.

SELECTED RESPONSE
Select the correct answer.

1. In the formula $B = B_0 e^{rt}$, B is the balance, in dollars, of an account with initial balance B_0 that earns interest at a decimal rate r compounded continuously for t years. How can you rewrite this formula to use it to find the number of years needed to attain a certain balance?

   Ⓐ $t = r \ln \dfrac{B}{B_0}$ ⊙Ⓒ $t = \dfrac{\ln B}{r \ln B_0}$

   Ⓑ $t = \ln \dfrac{B}{B_0} - r$ Ⓓ $t = \dfrac{1}{r} \ln \dfrac{B}{B_0}$

2. A small object with mass m is attached to a ceiling by a spring. The spring is pulled straight down and released so that the object begins to oscillate up and down. The period T of the object's oscillation is given by the formula $T = 2\pi \sqrt{\dfrac{m}{k}}$, where k is the spring constant, which describes the stiffness of the spring. Which of the following gives k as a function of m and T?

   Ⓐ $k = \dfrac{4\pi^2 \sqrt{m}}{T}$ Ⓒ $k = \dfrac{4\pi^2 m}{T^2}$

   Ⓑ $k = \dfrac{2\pi \sqrt{m}}{T}$ Ⓓ $k = \dfrac{2\pi m}{T^2}$

3. The volume V of a sphere is given by the formula $V = \dfrac{1}{6}\sqrt{\dfrac{S^3}{\pi}}$, where S is the surface area of the sphere. Which of the following gives S as a function of V?

   Ⓐ $S = \sqrt[3]{36\pi V^2}$

   Ⓑ $S = 36\pi \sqrt[3]{V^2}$

   Ⓒ $S = 6\pi \sqrt[3]{V^2}$

   Ⓓ $S = \sqrt[3]{6\pi V^2}$

Select all correct answers.

4. An object with mass m_1 and an object with mass m_2 whose centers of mass are a distance r apart experience an attractive gravitational force F given by the formula $F = \dfrac{Gm_1 m_2}{r^2}$, where G is the universal gravitational constant. Solve this formula for G, r, m_1, and m_2 to determine which equations given below are correct.

   Ⓐ $G = \dfrac{m_1 m_2 F}{r^2}$ Ⓔ $m_1 = \dfrac{Fr^2}{Gm_2}$

   Ⓑ $G = \dfrac{Fr^2}{m_1 m_2}$ Ⓕ $m_1 = \dfrac{FGm_2}{r^2}$

   Ⓒ $r = \sqrt{\dfrac{Gm_1 m_2}{F}}$ Ⓖ $m_2 = \dfrac{Fr^2}{Gm_1}$

   Ⓓ $r = \dfrac{Gm_1 m_2}{\sqrt{F}}$ Ⓗ $m_2 = \dfrac{FGm_1}{r^2}$

5. The power output P of a light bulb depends on the voltage V and current I in the circuit and is given by the formula $P = VI$. The voltage across the light bulb is dependent on the current running through it and the resistance R that the light bulb provides and is given by the formula $V = IR$. Solve the given formulas for their individual variables and combine them to determine which equations given below are correct.

   Ⓐ $V = \sqrt{RP}$ Ⓔ $R = \dfrac{P}{I^2}$

   Ⓑ $V = \sqrt{\dfrac{P}{R}}$ Ⓕ $R = \dfrac{P}{V^2}$

   Ⓒ $I = \sqrt{\dfrac{V}{PR}}$ Ⓖ $P = I^2 R$

   Ⓓ $I = \sqrt{\dfrac{P}{R}}$ Ⓗ $P = \dfrac{V^2}{R}$

CONSTRUCTED RESPONSE

6. An object off the ground has a *gravitational potential energy* that depends on its height above the ground. The energy is given by the formula $E = mgh$, where m is the object's mass, g is the acceleration due to gravity, and h is the object's height above the ground. If the object falls, the potential energy is transformed into *kinetic energy*, or the energy of motion. This energy is given by the formula $E = \frac{1}{2}mv^2$, where v is the velocity. By the law of conservation of energy, the total amount of energy of the falling object remains the same even though the form of the energy changes. Rearrange these formulas to write an equation for the object's velocity when it hits the ground as a function of the object's height above the ground before it falls. Show your work.

_____

_____

_____

7. The business leader of a toy-making company needs to determine the number n of employees that can be hired while maintaining a certain profit P. Employee wages are W dollars per day, and each employee will make t toys on average each day. Each product can be sold for S dollars and costs C dollars to produce. The daily overhead cost is H dollars. Write an equation for profit, explaining how you obtained the equation. Then find an equation expressing the number of employees that can be hired as a function of the other variables.

_____

_____

_____

8. A radioactive isotope will spontaneously decay into a more stable form. If a sample of the isotope initially contains N_0 radioactive atoms, the time t, in years, it takes until only N radioactive atoms remain in the sample is given by the formula $t = \frac{1}{k} \ln \frac{N_0}{N}$, where k is the radioactive decay constant of the isotope. The *half-life* of an isotope, denoted by $t_{0.5}$, is the time it takes for half of the atoms in a sample of the isotope to decay.

   a. Use the given formula to solve for the radioactive decay constant k as a function of half-life $t_{0.5}$. Show your work.

   _____

   _____

   b. Use your answer from part a to write an equation giving the number N of atoms of an isotope remaining in a sample as a function of time t and half-life $t_{0.5}$. Show your work.

   _____

   _____

   _____

9. A planet in an elliptical orbit with *semi-major axis R* around a star of mass M has an orbital period T approximated by the formula $T^2 = \frac{4\pi^2}{GM}R^3$, where G is the universal gravitational constant.

   Rearrange the formula to solve for the semi-major axis R. Show your work. If Jupiter has an orbital period of 11.86 Earth-years, about how many times farther away is it from the Sun than Earth is? (You can use the variable R as an approximation for the distance of a planet from a star.) Explain.

   _____

   _____

   _____

The student will explain each step in solving an equation and construct an argument to justify a solution method.

SELECTED RESPONSE

Select the correct answer.

1. Which property is NOT used to justify a step taken in solving the rational equation $\dfrac{2(x+8)}{x} = 10$?

$$\frac{2(x+8)}{x} = 10$$

$$\frac{2x+16}{x} = 10$$

$$\frac{2x+16}{x} \cdot x = 10 \cdot x$$

$$2x+16 = 10x$$

$$2x+16-2x = 10x-2x$$

$$16 = 8x$$

$$\frac{16}{8} = \frac{8x}{8}$$

$$2 = x$$

Ⓐ Zero product property

Ⓑ Addition/subtraction property of equality

Ⓒ Multiplication/division property of equality

Ⓓ Distributive property

Select all correct answers.

2. Circle each listed property that can be used to justify a step taken in solving the radical equation $3\sqrt{5x+6} = 18$.

$$3\sqrt{5x+6} = 18$$

$$\frac{3\sqrt{5x+6}}{3} = \frac{18}{3}$$

$$\sqrt{5x+6} = 6$$

$$\left(\sqrt{5x+6}\right)^2 = 6^2$$

$$5x+6 = 36$$

$$5x+6-6 = 36-6$$

$$5x = 30$$

$$\frac{5x}{5} = \frac{30}{5}$$

$$x = 6$$

Multiplication/division property of equality

Symmetric property of equality

Transitive property of equality

Addition/subtraction property of equality

Distributive property

Definition of square root

CONSTRUCTED RESPONSE

3. Write justifications for steps (2), (5), (7), and (8) in solving the equation $2x\sqrt{x}+5 = 21$.

(1)	$2x\sqrt{x}+5 = 21$	Given
(2)	$2x\sqrt{x}+5-5 = 21-5$	_____
(3)	$2x\sqrt{x} = 16$	Simplify.
(4)	$\left(2x\sqrt{x}\right)^2 = 16^2$	Square both sides.
(5)	$2^2 x^2\left(\sqrt{x}\right)^2 = 256$	_____
(6)	$4x^2(x) = 256$	Power of a power property
(7)	$4x^3 = 256$	_____
(8)	$\dfrac{4x^3}{4} = \dfrac{256}{4}$	_____
(9)	$x^3 = 64$	Simplify.
(10)	$\sqrt[3]{x^3} = \sqrt[3]{64}$	Take the cube root of both sides.
(11)	$x = 4$	Definition of cube root

4. Solve the equation $\dfrac{5x^2+4x+3}{x^2+2x-1}=6$.

   Justify the steps taken in the solution with the properties of equality and other mathematical properties. When needed, use "Given," "Simplify," and "Factor" as justifications.

   _____

   _____

   _____

   _____

   _____

   _____

   _____

   _____

5. Solve the equation $5 = 10\sqrt{1-\dfrac{x^2}{a^2}}$ for x in

   terms of a, where x and a are positive real numbers and $x < a$. Show your work, justifying each step. (Use the properties of equality, the distributive property, and properties of roots and exponents as justifications. Also use "Given" and "Simplify" when needed.)

   _____

   _____

   _____

   _____

   _____

   _____

   _____

6. Four runners form a relay team to compete in a 4 × 100 meter relay. Two of the runners run at a certain speed in meters per second, and the other two runners run 2 meters per second faster. If it takes a total of 70 seconds for the team to finish the race, how fast are the runners? Assume all speeds are constant, and round your answers to the nearest tenth. Show your work, justifying each step. When needed, use "Given" and "Simplify" as justifications. (Hint: Start with the equation $t = t_1 + t_2 + t_3 + t_4$ where the team time t equals the sum of the times of the individual runners.

   Remember that $t = \dfrac{d}{r}$, where d is

   distance run and r is the rate, or speed, of a runner.)

   _____

   _____

   _____

   _____

   _____

   _____

   _____

   _____

   _____

   _____

   _____

   _____

   _____

   _____

   _____

The student will solve rational and radical equations, and give examples showing how extraneous solutions may arise.

SELECTED RESPONSE

Select the correct answer.

1. Which equation has an extraneous solution that is negative?

    Ⓐ $\sqrt{5x+29} = x+7$

    Ⓑ $\dfrac{16}{x+10} = \dfrac{2x+36}{x+10}$

    Ⓒ $\sqrt{7x-5}+5 = x$

    Ⓓ $\dfrac{3}{x-8} = \dfrac{5x-34}{x^2-14x+48}$

2. For which of the following equations does solving algebraically lead to at least one extraneous solution?

    Ⓐ $\sqrt[3]{5x^2+6x} = x$

    Ⓑ $\dfrac{x+3}{x+5} = \dfrac{4}{x}$

    Ⓒ $\sqrt{x+8}-8 = x$

    Ⓓ $\dfrac{x}{x-3} + \dfrac{2}{x+5} = -\dfrac{16}{x^2+2x-15}$

Select all correct answers.

3. Rational expressions sometimes have excluded values because these values make the expression undefined. The excluded values can sometimes lead to extraneous solutions when solving an equation that contains the expression. Circle each rational expression that has excluded values.

    $\dfrac{x+6}{x^2-10x+24}$

    $\dfrac{5x^2-20}{6x+21}$

    $\dfrac{x^2-4x}{6}$

    $\dfrac{3}{x-2}$

    $\dfrac{x}{x^2+1}$

CONSTRUCTED RESPONSE

4. Solve the radical equation $\sqrt{2x+1}+7 = x$. Show your work. Remember to check for extraneous solutions.

    _____

    _____

    _____

    _____

    _____

    _____

    _____

5. Solve the rational equation $\dfrac{2x}{5} = -4 + \dfrac{x-1}{x+2}$. Show your work. Remember to check for extraneous solutions.

    _____

    _____

    _____

    _____

    _____

    _____

6. Josie solved the radical equation $\sqrt{-8x-16}-2 = x$ algebraically and said that the equation has two solutions: -2 and -10. Is Josie correct? Explain why or why not.

    _____

    _____

    _____

    _____

    _____

    _____

7. a. Show that the rational equation
$\dfrac{6}{2-x}+\dfrac{6}{2+x}=3$ has no solution.

_____

_____

_____

_____

_____

b. Given that the rational equation
$\dfrac{6}{2-x}+\dfrac{6}{2+x}=g$ has a solution of
$x=1$, find the value of g. Show
your work.

_____

_____

_____

_____

_____

c. Are there any other solutions of
the equation from part b? Show
your work.

_____

_____

_____

_____

_____

8. Give an example of a rational equation
that has an extraneous solution. Solve
the equation and explain why the
extraneous solution occurs.

_____

_____

_____

_____

_____

_____

_____

_____

9. Aaron incorrectly states that the only
solution of the radical equation $x=\sqrt{x}$
is 1. His work is shown below. Identify
Aaron's mistake. Describe two ways that
Aaron could have avoided his mistake.

$$x=\sqrt{x}$$
$$x^2=x$$
$$\dfrac{x^2}{x}=\dfrac{x}{x}$$
$$x=1$$

_____

_____

_____

_____

_____

_____

The student will solve quadratic equations by various methods and will recognize and write complex solutions.

SELECTED RESPONSE
Select the correct answer.

1. Which of the following quadratic equations has no real solutions?

    Ⓐ $x^2 + 3x - 5 = 0$

    Ⓑ $4x^2 + 4x + 1 = 0$

    Ⓒ $2x^2 - 4x + 3 = 0$

    Ⓓ $x^2 - 6x - 2 = 0$

2. Which equation below allows you to solve $2x^2 - 15 = x$ using the zero product property?

    Ⓐ $(2x + 5)(x - 3) = 0$

    Ⓑ $(2x - 5)(x - 3) = 0$

    Ⓒ $(2x + 5)(x + 3) = 0$

    Ⓓ $(2x - 5)(x + 3) = 0$

Select all correct answers.

3. Circle the quadratic equations that have non-real solutions.

    $x^2 + 3x - 25 = -7$

    $-x^2 + 7x + 1 = 13$

    $x^2 + 2x = -5$

    $2x^2 + x + 13 = 0$

    $-2x^2 + 4x + 9 = 11$

CONSTRUCTED RESPONSE

4. Solve each equation over the set of complex numbers. Write the solutions using the imaginary unit i as necessary.

    a. $x^2 - 16 = 0$

    _____

    b. $x^2 + 36 = 0$

    _____

    c. $x^2 - 17 = 0$

    _____

    d. $x^2 + 5 = 0$

5. Solve the equation $x^2 + 14x + 65 = -2$ over the set of complex numbers by completing the square. Show your work, and write the solutions using the imaginary unit i as necessary.

    _____

    _____

    _____

    _____

6. Consider the quadratic equation $3x^2 - 9x + 20 = 13$.

    a. What method should be used to most easily solve the equation over the set of complex numbers? Explain your reasoning.

    _____

    _____

    b. Solve the equation using the method from part a. Show your work, and write the solutions using the imaginary unit i as necessary.

    _____

    _____

    _____

    _____

7. Solve the equation $3x + 5 = \dfrac{8}{x}$, where $x \neq 0$. Show your work, and write the solutions using the imaginary unit i as necessary.

    _____

    _____

    _____

    _____

8. Consider the equation $kx^2 + 8x + 11 = 0$, where k is a nonzero real number.

   a. Find the values for k such that the equation has two non-real solutions. Show your work.

   _____

   _____

   _____

   b. Using the information from part a, find the values of k such that the equation has one real solution. Explain your reasoning.

   _____

   _____

   c. Using the information from part a, find the values of k such that the equation has two real solutions. Explain your reasoning.

   _____

   _____

   d. Find the solutions of the equation for the values of k from parts a, b, and c. Show your work, and write the solutions using the imaginary unit i as necessary.

   _____

   _____

   _____

   _____

9. Consider the quadratic equation $x^2 + bx = 4$, where b is a real number.

   a. For what values of b would you solve the equation by taking a square root? Explain.

   _____

   _____

   b. For what values of b would you solve the equation by factoring? Explain.

   _____

   _____

   c. For what values of b would you solve the equation by completing the square or using the quadratic formula? Explain.

   _____

   _____

   _____

The student will solve systems of linear equations in two variables exactly and approximately (e.g., with graphs).

SELECTED RESPONSE
Select the correct answer.

1. Circle the system that makes a true statement.

   A system of equations that is equivalent to the system
   $$\begin{cases} 3x + y - 2z = 18 \\ 4x - 3y + 5z = 9 \\ -5x + 2y - z = -13 \end{cases}$$

   is

   $$\begin{cases} -2x + 3y - 3z = 5 \\ 4x - 3y + 5z = 9 \\ -5x + 2y - z = -13 \end{cases}$$

   $$\begin{cases} -x - y + 4z = -4 \\ 4x - 3y + 5z = 9 \\ -5x + 2y - z = -13 \end{cases}$$

   $$\begin{cases} 3x + y - 2z = 18 \\ 4x - 3y + 5z = 9 \\ 7x - 2y + 3z = 27 \end{cases}$$

   $$\begin{cases} 3x + y - 2z = 18 \\ -2x + 3y - 3z = 5 \\ -5x + 2y - z = -13 \end{cases}$$

2. Given the following system of equations, what number should you multiply the first equation by so that the *x*-term will be eliminated when the first equation is added to the second equation?
   $$\begin{cases} 2x - y + 7z = 65 \\ -3x + 4y - 2z = -5 \\ x + 9y - 5z = -24 \end{cases}$$

   Ⓐ $-\dfrac{3}{2}$

   Ⓑ $-\dfrac{2}{3}$

   Ⓒ $\dfrac{2}{3}$

   Ⓓ $\dfrac{3}{2}$

3. Which of the following equations would result in a system having one solution if grouped with the two equations below?
   $$\begin{cases} 3x + y - 2z = 18 \\ 4x - 3y + 5z = 9 \\ \quad\quad ? \end{cases}$$

   Ⓐ $-x + 4y - 7z = 9$

   Ⓑ $9x + 3y - 6z = 54$

   Ⓒ $-5x + 2y - z = -13$

   Ⓓ $4x - 3y + 5z = 12$

CONSTRUCTED RESPONSE

4. Does the system of equations below have one solution, infinitely many solutions, or no solution? Explain.
   $$\begin{cases} -3x + 24y + 9z = -111 \\ x - 8y - 3z = 37 \\ 2x - 16y - 6z = 75 \end{cases}$$

   _____

   _____

   _____

5. Given the following system of equations, solve for *x*, *y*, and *z*. Show your work.
   $$\begin{cases} 2x + 3y + z = 27 \\ x + 5y - 3z = 52 \\ -3x + y + 2z = -16 \end{cases}$$

   _____

   _____

   _____

   _____

   _____

   _____

   _____

   _____

6. Consider the system of equations below.
$$\begin{cases} 3x + 5y - 2z = -7 \\ -2x + 7y + 6z = -3 \\ 8x + 3y - 10z = -11 \end{cases}$$

   a. Explain why the system has infinitely many solutions.

   _____

   _____

   b. Write the generalized form of the solution and express the values for x and y in terms of z. Show your work.

   _____

   _____

   _____

   _____

   _____

   _____

   _____

7. Danielle and Inder brought apples, bananas, and oranges to a fruit sale. The bananas were sold for $0.50 each, while the apples and oranges were sold for $0.75 each. They sold 50 pieces of fruit and earned $33.50 total. If Danielle and Inder sold twice as many bananas as oranges, how many apples did they sell? Show your work.

   _____

   _____

   _____

   _____

   _____

   _____

8. A small business has three employees who decorate pastries. Carlotta earns $11 per hour and decorates 12 pastries each hour on average. James earns $10 per hour and decorates 11 pastries each hour on average. Melissa was recently employed and earns $8 per hour. She decorates 7 pastries each hour on average. In one week, the employees worked for 96 total hours, decorated 1016 pastries, and earned a total of $960 in wages. How many hours did each employee work? Show your work.

   _____

   _____

   _____

   _____

   _____

   _____

   _____

9. Dining room sets consisting of armchairs, side chairs, and a table are sold at a local furniture store. A set with 2 armchairs, 4 side chairs, and a table is sold for $940. A set with 4 side chairs and a table is sold for $740. A set with 4 armchairs, 2 side chairs, and a table is sold for $1020. What are the individual prices of an armchair, a side chair, and a table? How would you spend a budget of $900 to buy a dining room set?

   _____

   _____

   _____

   _____

   _____

   _____

The student will solve a linear-quadratic system in two variables algebraically and graphically.

SELECTED RESPONSE

Select the correct answer.

1. What is the distance between the points of intersection of the graphs of $y = x^2$ and $y = 6 - x$?

   Ⓐ $\sqrt{26}$

   Ⓑ $5\sqrt{2}$

   Ⓒ $2\sqrt{37}$

   Ⓓ $\sqrt{170}$

2. Circle the number that makes a true statement.

   The number of times that the graphs of $y = -x^2 + 5x + 6$ and $2x + y = 16$

   intersect is $\boxed{\begin{matrix} 0 \\ 1 \\ 2 \\ 3 \end{matrix}}$.

Select all correct answers.

3. Which of the following systems of equations have at least one solution in Quadrant I?

   Ⓐ $\begin{cases} -4x + 3y = 1 \\ y = x^2 - x + 1 \end{cases}$

   Ⓑ $\begin{cases} x - 3y = 2 \\ y = x^2 + 2x - 34 \end{cases}$

   Ⓒ $\begin{cases} 3x + y = -2 \\ y = x^2 - 2x - 4 \end{cases}$

   Ⓓ $\begin{cases} 2x + y = -1 \\ y = -x^2 - 6x - 5 \end{cases}$

   Ⓔ $\begin{cases} x + y = 3 \\ y = x^2 - 8x + 16 \end{cases}$

CONSTRUCTED RESPONSE

4. Find all the points of intersection between the line $2x + y = 4$ and the ellipse $\dfrac{x^2}{4} + \dfrac{y^2}{16} = 1$. Show your work.

   _____
   _____
   _____
   _____
   _____
   _____
   _____
   _____
   _____
   _____
   _____
   _____

5. Graph the following system of equations and then solve the system graphically.

   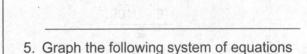

   $\begin{cases} 2x + y = -12 \\ y = x^2 - 5 \end{cases}$

   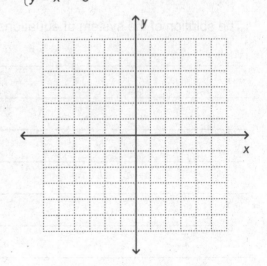

6. Graph the following system of equations and then solve the system graphically.

$$\begin{cases} -5x + y = 5 \\ x - y^2 = -1 \end{cases}$$

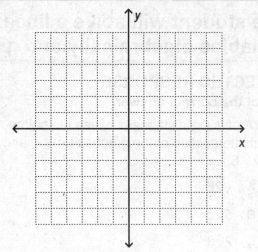

7. Terrell was asked to find the solution(s) of the system of equations $\begin{cases} y = -2x - 5 \\ y = x^2 + 4x - 21 \end{cases}$.

His work and graph are shown. Once Terrell graphed the system of equations to check his answer, he knew he had made a mistake somewhere. State how Terrell knew he made a mistake, identify the mistake, and find the correct solution(s) of the system of equations. Show your work.

$x^2 + 4x - 21 = -2x - 5$

$x^2 + 6x - 16 = 0$

$$x = \frac{-6 + \sqrt{36 - 4(1)(-16)}}{2}$$

$$= \frac{-6 + \sqrt{100}}{2}$$

$$= \frac{-6 + 10}{2}$$

$$= 2$$

$y = -2(2) - 5 = -9$

The solution of the system of equations is (2, –9).

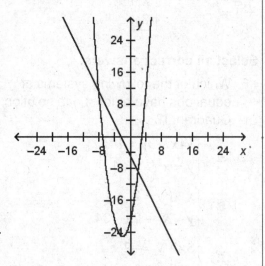

The student will use intersection(s) of the graphs of *f(x)* and *g(x)* to approximate solution(s) of the equation *f(x)* = *g(x)*.

SELECTED RESPONSE
Select the correct answer.

1. Use the graph below to determine which of the following is the best approximation of the solutions of the equation $f(x) = g(x)$.

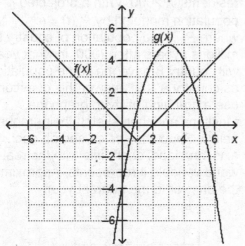

A) $x = -1, x = 5$

B) $x = -0.5, x = 2.5$

C) $x = 0.5, x = 4.5$

D) $x = 1, x = 3$

2. Use the table below to determine which of the following is the best approximation of the solution of the equation $f(x) = g(x)$ if $f(x) = \dfrac{1}{x} + 1$ and $g(x) = \sqrt{x}$.

x	f(x)	g(x)
0.5	3	0.71
1	2	1
1.5	1.67	1.22
2	1.5	1.41
2.5	1.4	1.58
3	1.33	1.73

A) $x = 2.5$

B) $x = 2$

C) $x = 1.5$

D) $x = 1$

Select all correct answers.

3. Use the graphs of $f(x)$ and $g(x)$ to determine all of the solutions of the equation $f(x) = g(x)$. Approximate to the nearest integer. Circle each correct answer.

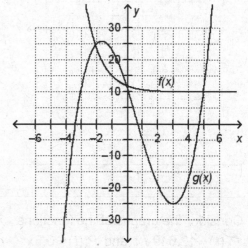

$x = -3$	$x = 3$	$x = 12$
$x = -2$	$x = 5$	$x = 15$
$x = 0$	$x = 10$	$x = 25$

CONSTRUCTED RESPONSE

4. Consider the functions $f(x) = -|x - 2| + 5$ and $g(x) = 2\sqrt{x} + 1$. The following table lists the values of $f(x)$ and $g(x)$ for integer values of x from 0 to 6. Use the table to approximate the solution of the equation $f(x) = g(x)$ to the nearest integer. Justify your answer.

x	f(x)	g(x)
0	3	1
1	4	3
2	5	3.83
3	4	4.46
4	3	5
5	2	5.47
6	1	5.90

_____

_____

_____

5. Graph the functions $f(x) = |x + 2| - 3$ and $g(x) = \dfrac{1}{x + 1}$. Approximate the solution(s) of the equation $f(x) = g(x)$ to the nearest 0.5 unit.

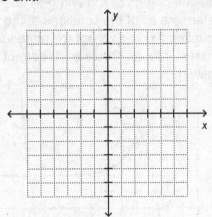

_____

_____

6. Consider the graphs of the functions $P_A(t) = 12.649\sqrt{x}$ and $P_B(t) = 0.5x^2$ shown. If $P_A(t)$ models the annual profit P_A, in thousands of dollars, of business A as a function of time t, in years, while $P_B(t)$ models the annual profit P_B, in thousands of dollars, of business B as a function of time t, in years, what is the significance of the points where the graphs of $P_A(t)$ and $P_B(t)$ intersect? Estimate the t-coordinate of these points to the nearest 0.5 year.

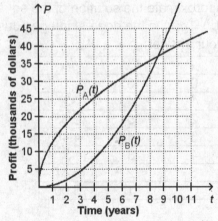

7. Two small countries have two different population growth rates. Country A had 23 million residents in 2000 and a projected population modeled by $P_A(t) = 0.0096t^2 + 0.997t + 23$, where P_A is the population of country A in millions and t is time in years after 2000. Country B is a prosperous country that attracts many immigrants but only had 17 million residents in 2000. With a projected population modeled by $P_B(t) = e^{0.1t} + 17$, where P_B is the population of country B in millions t years after 2000, in what year will country B have the same population as country A? To answer this question, use a graphing utility to graph the functions and then sketch their graphs below. Show the scale used on each axis, and label each axis with the real-world variable it represents. Approximate the answer to the nearest year.

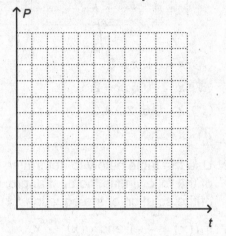

_____

_____

The student will interpret key features of graphs and tables, and sketch graphs showing key features given a description.

SELECTED RESPONSE
Select the correct answer.

1. Circle the phrase that makes a true statement.

   The table shows the time, in years, it takes for an interest-bearing account to double in value when the annual interest rate is r%. The statement that best describes the doubling-time function is:

The doubling-time function is a constant function.
The doubling-time function is an increasing function.
The doubling-time function is a decreasing function.
There is no pattern in the behavior of the doubling-time function.

Interest rate	Doubling time (years)
1%	69.7
2%	35.0
3%	23.5
4%	17.7
5%	14.2
6%	11.9
7%	10.2
8%	9.0

Select all correct answers.

2. A small object at rest on a frictionless surface is attached to a wall by a frictionless spring. The object is pulled away from the wall to stretch the spring and then released. The graph shows the displacement d, in centimeters, of the object from its resting position as a function of time t, in seconds, as the object oscillates. Which of the following statements are true?

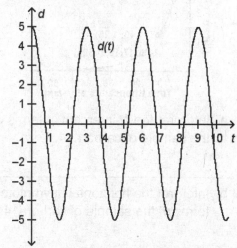

Ⓐ The d-intercept indicates that the spring was initially stretched 5 cm.

Ⓑ The d-intercept indicates that the spring was initially stretched 10 cm.

Ⓒ The time it takes for the spring to return to its initial stretched position is 1.5 seconds.

Ⓓ The time it takes for the spring to return to its initial stretched position is 3 seconds.

Ⓔ The t-intercepts are the times when the spring is compressed.

Ⓕ The t-intercepts are the times when the spring is stretched.

Ⓖ The t-coordinates of the minimum points are the times when the spring is fully stretched.

Ⓗ The t-coordinates of the minimum points are the times when the spring is fully compressed.

CONSTRUCTED RESPONSE

3. Radioactive isotopes such as carbon-14 spontaneously decay into more stable atoms. The graph shows the number N, in billions, of atoms of carbon-14 in a sample as a function of time t, in thousands of years.

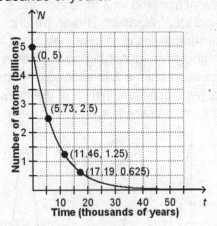

a. Interpret the N-intercept in terms of the sample of carbon-14.

_____

b. Interpret the horizontal asymptote in terms of the sample of carbon-14.

_____

c. The *half-life* of a radioactive isotope is the time it takes for one half of a sample to decay. What is the half-life of carbon-14?

_____

4. The table of values below gives the probability function P(n) of getting all 5s when rolling a number cube n times.

n	1	2	3	4	5
P(n)	$\dfrac{1}{6}$	$\dfrac{1}{36}$	$\dfrac{1}{216}$	$\dfrac{1}{1296}$	$\dfrac{1}{7776}$

a. Is P(n) increasing or decreasing? Explain the significance of this fact.

_____

b. What is the end behavior of P(n)? Explain the significance of this fact.

_____

5. The graph shows a function that models the value V, in millions of dollars, of a stock portfolio as a function of time t, in months, over an 18-month period.

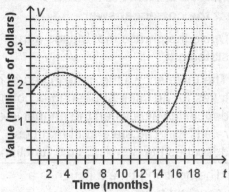

a. For what values of t is the function increasing? For what values of t is the function decreasing? Approximate the endpoints of the intervals to the nearest 0.5 month.

_____

b. Interpret the intervals found in part a in terms of the situation.

_____

c. Identify the coordinates of any local maximums and local minimums. Approximate the t-values to the nearest 0.5 month and the V-values to the nearest 0.25 million dollars.

_____

d. Explain the significance of any local maximums and minimums in part c.

_____

e. What does the fact that the function is always positive indicate about the appropriateness of this model?

_____

Name _____ Date _____ Class_____

The student will relate the domain of a function to its graph and to any quantitative relationship it describes.

SELECTED RESPONSE
Select the correct answer.

1. The graph of a logarithmic function is shown. What is the domain of the function?

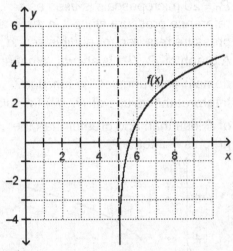

  Ⓐ $x \geq 5$ Ⓒ $-\infty < y < \infty$

  Ⓑ $x > 5$ Ⓓ $y < 5$

2. The graph of a fourth-degree polynomial function $f(x)$ is shown. Use the graph to determine the domain and range of $f(x)$.

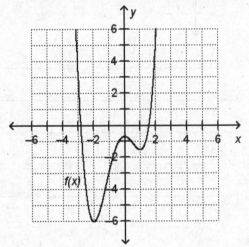

  Ⓐ Domain: $-\infty < x < \infty$; range: $f(x) \geq -6$

  Ⓑ Domain: $-\infty < x < \infty$;
     range: $-\infty < f(x) < \infty$

  Ⓒ Domain: $-4 < x < 2$; range: $f(x) \geq -6$

  Ⓓ Domain: $-4 < x < 2$;
     range: $-\infty < f(x) < \infty$

3. A cosine function models the angular displacement θ, in degrees, of a frictionless pendulum as a function of the time t, in seconds, since the pendulum starts to swing. What is the domain of this function?

  Ⓐ $-\infty < t < \infty$ Ⓒ $t > 0$

  Ⓑ $-1 \leq t \leq 1$ Ⓓ $t \geq 0$

Select all correct answers.

4. Determine the intervals that are in the domain of the piecewise-defined function $f(x)$.

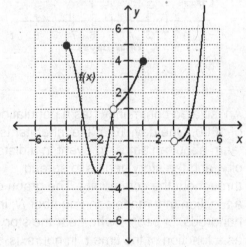

  Ⓐ $-4 \leq x \leq -1$ Ⓔ $1 < x < 3$

  Ⓑ $-4 \leq x < -1$ Ⓕ $1 \leq x < 3$

  Ⓒ $-1 < x \leq 1$ Ⓖ $x > 3$

  Ⓓ $-1 < x < 1$ Ⓗ $x \geq 3$

CONSTRUCTED RESPONSE

5. The number of possible combinations of heads and tails in a series of coin flips depends on the number n of coins that are flipped, and it is given by the function $C(n) = 2^n$. What is the domain of the function $C(n)$? Explain. Is the graph of $C(n)$ continuous or discrete? Explain.

_____

_____

_____

6. The square root function $h(t)$ graphed below models the height h, in centimeters, of a certain type of plant t days after sprouting. What are the domain and range of $h(t)$? Is there a practical limit to the values in the domain, beyond which the model is not appropriate? Explain.

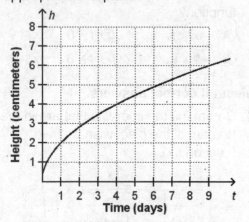

Time (days)

7. An isolated community has a population of 1000. One day, 10 of the inhabitants learn about an amusing event in a distant city, and the story begins to spread throughout the community. The graph of a function that models the number N, in hundreds, of people who hear the story as a function of the time t, in hours, is shown. What are the domain and range of $N(t)$? Describe why this model is not appropriate for large values of t.

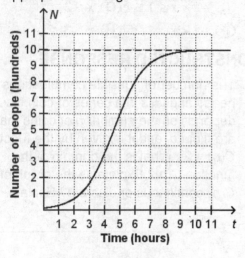

Time (hours)

8. The unit *decibel* (dB) is typically used when relating sound pressure to human hearing. The pressure of sound P_{dB}, in decibels, is given by the function

$$P_{dB}(P) = 10 \log \frac{P}{P_0},$$ where P is the sound pressure in micropascals and P_0 is a reference pressure in micropascals. $P_0 = 20$ micropascals is used as a reference pressure since it is the average pressure required for audible sound. A graph of $P_{dB}(P)$ is shown. What are the domain and range of the function? Interpret the values of $P_{dB}(P)$ for values of P less than and greater than the graph's P-intercept.

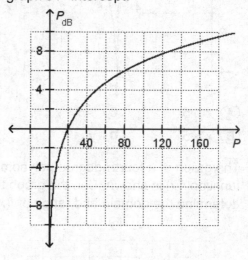

_____

_____

_____

_____

_____

The student will use symbols or a table to find the average rate of change of functions and estimate rates from graphs.

SELECTED RESPONSE

Select the correct answer.

1. The table shows the population of a colony of bacteria at the beginning of each week for five weeks. During which week was the average rate of change in population 873 bacteria per day?

Week	Population
1	600
2	1260
3	2650
4	5560
5	11,671

(A) Week 1

(B) Week 2

(C) Week 3

(D) Week 4

2. On which of the following intervals is the average rate of change of the function $f(x) = x^3 - 4x$ the greatest?

(A) From $x = -3$ to $x = -1$

(B) From $x = -1$ to $x = 1$

(C) From $x = 1$ to $x = 3$

(D) From $x = 3$ to $x = 5$

Select all correct answers.

3. The table shows some values of a polynomial function. Over which intervals is the average rate of change of the function positive?

x	0	1	2	3
f(x)	50	75	40	65

(A) From $x = 0$ to $x = 1$

(B) From $x = 0$ to $x = 2$

(C) From $x = 0$ to $x = 3$

(D) From $x = 1$ to $x = 2$

(E) From $x = 1$ to $x = 3$

(F) From $x = 2$ to $x = 3$

Using the list of numbers at the right, write the rate of change for each given interval on the graph of the function.

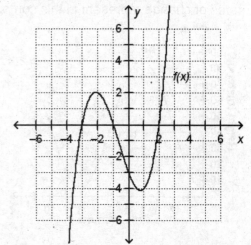

4. From $x = -3$ to $x = -2$ [ ]

5. From $x = -2$ to $x = 1$ [ ]

6. From $x = 0$ to $x = 1$ [ ]

7. From $x = 1$ to $x = 2$ [ ]

8. From $x = -1$ to $x = 0$ [ ]

9. From $x = -1$ to $x = 2$ [ ]

-3
-2
-1
0
1
2
3
4

CONSTRUCTED RESPONSE

10. A sphere with diameter d, in feet, is inside a cube with edge length d. The volume V, in cubic feet, of the interior of the cube that is not occupied by the sphere is given by the polynomial function $V(d) = \left(\dfrac{6 - \pi}{6}\right) d^3$. Find, to the nearest integer, the average rate of change of the function over the interval $2 \le d \le 3$. Show your work.

_____

_____

11. The graph shows the height h, in meters, of a passenger on a Ferris wheel as a function of the time t, in minutes, since the ride began. Find the average rate of change of $h(t)$ over the intervals $0 \leq t \leq 4$ and $4 \leq t \leq 8$. What do these average rates of change represent in this context?

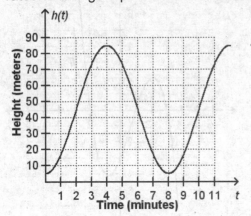

_____

_____

12. The logarithmic function $h(a)$ models the recommended chair seat height h, in inches, for a child whose age is a, in years. The graph of $h(a)$ is shown. Estimate the average rate of change of the function over the interval $6 \leq a \leq 10$. Show your work. What does the average rate of change represent in this context?

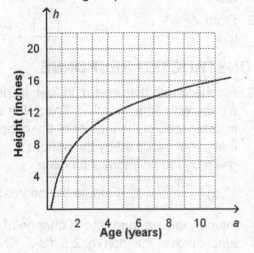

_____

_____

13. Erica made the following conjecture about average rates of change.

> The average rate of change of a function $f(x)$ defined for all x on the interval $a \leq x \leq c$ is equal to the mean of the average rates of change of $f(x)$ on the subintervals $a \leq x \leq b$ and $b \leq x \leq c$, where b is a number between a and c.

a. Show that Erica's conjecture is true for the function $f(x) = x^2$ when the interval is $0 \leq x \leq 4$ and the subintervals are $0 \leq x \leq 2$ and $2 \leq x \leq 4$.

_____

_____

_____

b. Using the function $f(x) = x^2$ and the interval $0 \leq x \leq 4$, find subintervals $0 \leq x \leq b$ and $b \leq x \leq 4$ for which Erica's conjecture is false. Then show that the conjecture is false.

_____

_____

_____

_____

c. By restricting the value of b, modify Erica's conjecture so that it is always true. Then prove the modified statement. Your proof should not use a specific function or specific values of a, b, and c.

_____

_____

_____

_____

_____

The student will graph functions: square root, cube root, and piecewise-defined, including step and absolute value.

SELECTED RESPONSE
Select the correct answer.

1. The graph shows the radius r of a ball bearing with uniform density as a function of its mass m. What type of function best describes the graph?

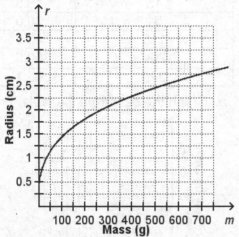

Ⓐ Quadratic function

Ⓑ Cubic function

Ⓒ Cube root function

Ⓓ Square root function

2. The graph of which function is shown?

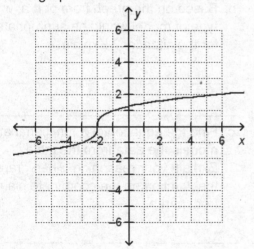

Ⓐ $y = \sqrt{x+2}$

Ⓑ $y = \sqrt{x-2}$

Ⓒ $y = \sqrt[3]{x+2}$

Ⓓ $y = \sqrt[3]{x-2}$

Select all correct answers.

3. The graph of the piecewise-defined function $f(x)$ is shown. Which of the following statements are true?

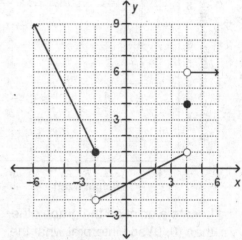

Ⓐ The y-intercept is 2.

Ⓑ The y-intercept is -1.

Ⓒ The domain is all real numbers.

Ⓓ The range is all real numbers.

Ⓔ $f(x)$ is undefined at $x = 4$.

CONSTRUCTED RESPONSE

4. Consider the function $y = 2\sqrt{x+2} + 4$.

   a. Graph the function.

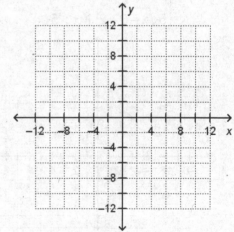

   b. What are the domain and range of the function?

   _____

Name _____ Date _____ Class_____

5. The function $d(h) = 1.2\sqrt{h}$ models the distance d, in miles, to the horizon for a person whose eye level is at height h, in feet, above the ground.

a. Graph the function.

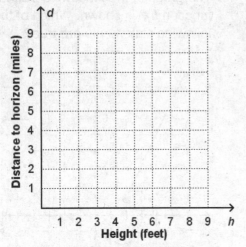

b. Locate a point on the graph other than (0, 0) and interpret what the coordinates of that point mean in the context of the situation.

_____

6. Graph the piecewise-defined function $f(x)$ given below. Then describe the function's domain and range and any intercepts that the graph has.

$$f(x) = \begin{cases} -2x - 2 & \text{if } x < 2 \\ 2 & \text{if } 2 \le x \le 5 \\ 5\sqrt{x-5} + 2 & \text{if } x > 5 \end{cases}$$

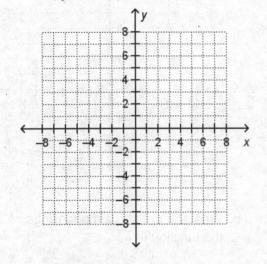

7. When investigating car accidents, experts deduce the speed a car was traveling from the length of the skid marks the car made when braking. The table below relates speed s, in miles per hour, to the length ℓ, in feet, of the skid marks.

Length of skid marks (feet)	Speed (mi/h)
0	0
15	16.3
51	30.0
115	45.0
204	60.0
240	65.1

a. Graph the data from the table.

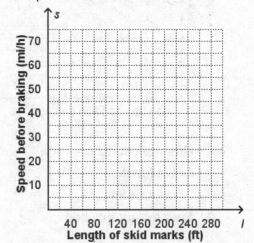

b. Based on the graph from part a, what type of model would be appropriate for the situation? Explain.

_____

_____

c. Find the equation of a function that models the data from the table. Explain your reasoning. Then graph the function on the coordinate plane from part a.

_____

d. Approximate the speed a car was traveling if the length of the skid marks is 40 feet. Round to the nearest mile per hour.

_____

Name _____ Date _____ Class_____

The student will graph polynomial functions, identify zeros using factorization if available, and show end behavior.

SELECTED RESPONSE
Select the correct answer.

1. Circle the function that makes a true statement. The graph of

$$p(x) = -(x - 1)(x + 1)(x + 4)$$
$$p(x) = (x + 1)(x - 1)(x - 4)$$
$$p(x) = -(x + 1)(x - 1)(x - 4)$$
$$p(x) = (x - 1)(x + 1)(x + 4)$$

is shown.

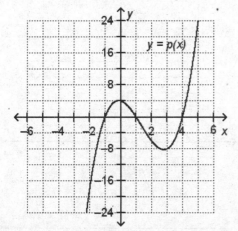

2. The graph of the polynomial function $p(x)$ is shown. What are the zeros of $p(x)$? (The zeros of $p(x)$ are integers, and the graph of $p(x)$ does not cross the x-axis at places other than those shown.)

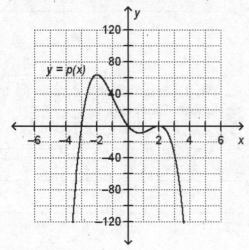

Ⓐ $x = -3$ and $x = 2$
Ⓑ $x = -3$, $x = 0$, and $x = 2$
Ⓒ $x = 0$
Ⓓ $x = -2$, $x = 0$, and $x = 3$

Select all correct answers.

3. Which of the following statements are true about the polynomial function $p(x)$? (The zeros of $p(x)$ are integers, and the graph of $p(x)$ does not cross the x-axis at places other than those shown.)

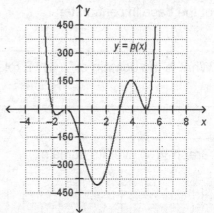

Ⓐ The degree of $p(x)$ is even.
Ⓑ The degree of $p(x)$ is 4.
Ⓒ The leading coefficient of $p(x)$ is negative.
Ⓓ The degree of $p(x)$ is at least 6.
Ⓔ $p(x)$ has four distinct zeros.

CONSTRUCTED RESPONSE

4. Identify the zeros of the polynomial function $p(x) = -x^3 - x^2 + 16x + 16$, and describe the function's end behavior. Then graph the function using the zeros and the end behavior and plotting any additional points as needed.

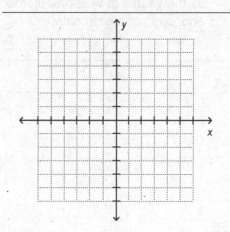

Name _____ Date _____ Class _____

5. The perimeter of the base of a right rectangular pyramid is 20 centimeters. The height of the pyramid equals $\frac{3}{5}$ of the product of the width and length of the base.

   a. Write a simplified equation for the volume V, in cubic centimeters, of the pyramid as a function of w, the width of the base in centimeters.

   _____

   b. What is the domain of $V(w)$? Explain.

   _____

   _____

   c. Graph $V(w)$ over its domain.

   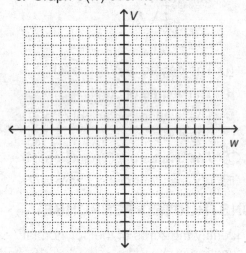

   d. What is the maximum volume of the pyramid?

   _____

   e. Describe the volume of the pyramid as the values of w approach the endpoints of the domain.

   _____

   _____

6. The function $T(t) = 0.04t^4 - 1.16t^3 + 9.93t^2 - 22.19t + 50.32$ models the average monthly high temperature T, in degrees Fahrenheit, of a city t months after January 1.

   a. Use a graphing utility to graph the function and then sketch the graph on the coordinate plane below. Describe the function's end behavior based on the graph.

   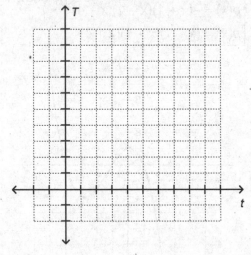

   _____

   _____

   b. Does the end behavior make sense in this context? Explain.

   _____

   _____

   _____

   c. What is a reasonable domain for this function? Explain.

   _____

   _____

   _____

The student will graph exponential, logarithmic, and trigonometric functions, showing key features of the graph.

SELECTED RESPONSE
Select the correct answer.

1. Circle the term that makes a true statement. Suppose a sheet of paper is repeatedly folded in half. The function $A(n) = A_0 \left(\dfrac{1}{2}\right)^n$ models the area of the sheet of paper after n folds. The A-intercept of the graph of $A(n)$ is

   $\begin{array}{c} 0 \\ \dfrac{1}{2} \\ n \\ A_0 \end{array}$.

2. What is the end behavior of the exponential function $f(x)$?

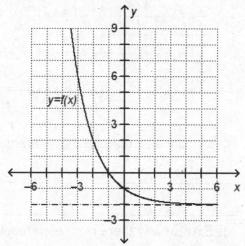

   (A) As x approaches $-\infty$, $f(x)$ approaches $-\infty$. As x approaches ∞, $f(x)$ approaches ∞.

   (B) As x approaches $-\infty$, $f(x)$ approaches ∞. As x approaches ∞, $f(x)$ approaches, but never reaches, -2.

   (C) As x decreases toward -4, $f(x)$ approaches ∞. As x approaches ∞, $f(x)$ approaches, but never reaches, -2.

   (D) As x approaches $-\infty$, $f(x)$ approaches ∞. As x approaches ∞, $f(x)$ approaches $-\infty$.

3. What y-intercept does the graph of the logarithmic function $f(x)$ have?

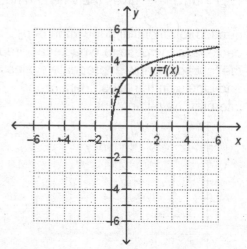

   (A) -1 (C) 3

   (B) 0 (D) 6

4. The graph of a cosine function is shown. What are the period, midline, and amplitude of the graph?

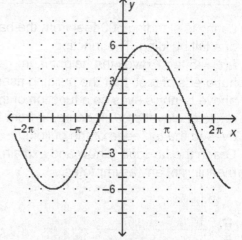

   (A) Period: 2π; midline: $y = 0$; amplitude: 12

   (B) Period: 2π; midline: $x = 0$; amplitude: 6

   (C) Period: 4π; midline: $y = 0$; amplitude: 6

   (D) Period: 4π; midline: $x = \dfrac{\pi}{2}$; amplitude: 6

CONSTRUCTED RESPONSE

5. The population of a certain type of bacteria doubles each hour. The function

   $t(p) = \log_2\left(\dfrac{p}{p_0}\right)$ gives the time t, in hours,

   needed for an initial population of p_0 bacteria to increase to p bacteria. Graph the function. Show appropriate scales and labels on the axes. Identify and interpret the p-intercept.

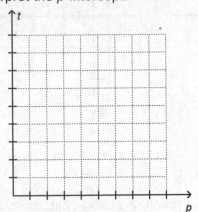

6. Lenny is standing 500 feet from the base of a tall building. The function $h(\theta) = 5 \tan \theta$ gives the height h, in hundreds of feet, that the building rises above Lenny's eyes as a function of the angle of elevation θ, in degrees, from his eyes to the top edge of the building. Graph the function. Show and explain the meaning of any asymptotes.

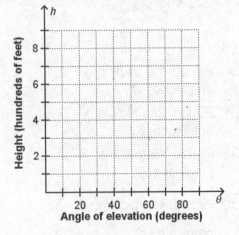

7. The owner of a small business purchases a new forklift for $31,000. If the value of the forklift depreciates at a rate of 15% per year, the function $V(t) = 31(0.85)^t$ models the value V, in thousands of dollars, of the forklift at time t, in years after its purchase.

   a. What are the domain and range of the function $V(t)$?

   _____

   b. Graph $V(t)$ over its domain. Show appropriate scales and labels on the axes.

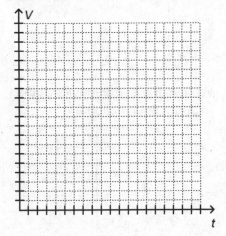

   c. Identify and interpret the V-intercept.

   _____

   _____

   d. Explain why there is no t-intercept.

   _____

   _____

   e. When the forklift's value falls to $2000, it is sold for scrap. Describe how the graph in part b would change to reflect this fact. Also, find the length of the forklift's useful life to the business.

   _____

   _____

The student will use the properties of exponents to interpret expressions for exponential functions.

SELECTED RESPONSE
Select the correct answer.

1. The balance B, in dollars, after t years of an investment that earns interest compounded annually is given by the function $B(t) = 1500(1.045)^t$. To the nearest hundredth of a percent, what is the monthly interest rate for the investment?

   (A) 0.37%   (C) 4.50%

   (B) 3.67%   (D) 69.59%

2. After t days, the mass m, in grams, of 100 grams of a certain radioactive element is given by the function $m(t) = 100(0.97)^t$. To the nearest percent, what is the weekly decay rate of the element?

   (A) 3%   (C) 21%

   (B) 19%   (D) 81%

Select all correct answers.

3. Which of these functions describe exponential growth?

   (A) $f(t) = 1.25^t$

   (B) $f(t) = 2(0.93)^{0.5t}$

   (C) $f(t) = 3(1.07)^{3t}$

   (D) $f(t) = 18(0.85)^t$

   (E) $f(t) = 0.5(1.05)^t$

   (F) $f(t) = 3(1.71)^{5t}$

   (G) $f(t) = 0.68^{2t}$

   (H) $f(t) = 8(1.56)^{1.4t}$

4. Indicate whether if each function is equivalent to $f(t) = 0.25^t$ by putting a check mark in the appropriate column of the table.

	Equivalent	Not equivalent
$f(t) = 1^{\frac{t}{4}}$		
$f(t) = 0.5^{2t}$		
$f(t) = 0.0625^{\frac{t}{2}}$		
$f(t) = 0.125^{\frac{t}{2}}$		
$f(t) = 4^{-t}$		
$f(t) = -0.25^{-t}$		

CONSTRUCTED RESPONSE

5. The population P, in millions, of a certain country can be modeled by the function $P(t) = 3.98(1.02)^t$, where t is the number of years after 1990.

   a. Write the equation in the form $P(t) = a(1 + r)^t$.

   _____

   b. What is the value of r in your answer from part a? What does this value represent?

   _____

   _____

6. How do the function values of $g(x) = 200(4^{x-1})$ compare to the corresponding function values of $f(x) = 200(4^x)$? Explain using a transformation of $g(x)$.

_____

_____

_____

_____

_____

_____

_____

_____

7. The value V, in dollars, after t years of an investment that earns interest compounded annually is given by the function $V(t) = 1500(1.035)^t$.

a. Rewrite $V(t)$ to find the annual interest rate of the investment.

_____

_____

_____

_____

b. Find the approximate interest rate over a 5-year period by rewriting the function using the power of a power property. Round to the nearest percent.

_____

_____

_____

8. Sanjay plans to deposit $850 in a bank account whose balance B, in dollars, after t years is modeled by $B(t) = 850(1.04)^t$.

a. Write the equation in the form $B(t) = a(1 + r)^t$. What is the annual interest rate of Sanjay's account?

_____

_____

_____

_____

_____

_____

b. Rewrite the equation from part a to approximate the monthly interest rate. Round to the nearest hundredth of a percent.

_____

_____

_____

_____

_____

_____

_____

c. Rebecca deposits $850 in a bank account that earns 0.35% interest compounded monthly. Without calculating the account balances, which account will have a larger balance after 6 months? Explain.

_____

_____

_____

_____

Name _____ Date _____ Class_____

The student will compare functions represented differently (algebraically, graphically, in tables, or by description).

SELECTED RESPONSE
Select the correct answer.

1. Which function has the same *y*-intercept as the function whose graph is shown?

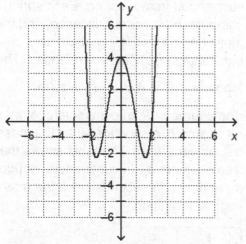

- (A) $f(x) = 2x^3 - 5x^2 + 3x - 4$
- (B) $f(x) = 3x^3 - 2x^2 + 5x + 4$
- (C) $f(x) = 2x^3 + x^2 - x - 2$
- (D) $f(x) = -2x^3 - x^2 + x + 2$

2. Which function has the same end behavior as the function whose graph is shown? (Assume that all key behavior is shown.)

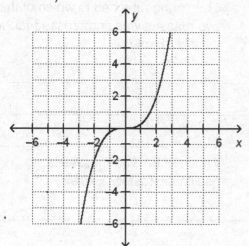

- (A) $f(x) = 2^x$
- (B) $f(x) = -10x^5 + 3x$
- (C) $f(x) = 2x^5 + 5x^3 - 4x^2 + 10$
- (D) $f(x) = x^4$

Select all correct answers.

3. Circle each function that shares at least one zero with the function whose graph is shown. (The zeros of the graphed function are integers, and the graphed function does not cross the *x*-axis at places other than those shown.)

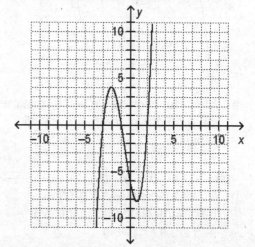

$f(x) = x^4 + x^3 - 7x^2 - x + 6$

$f(x) = x^3 - 2x^2 - 5x + 6$

$f(x) = x^2 + x - 6$

$f(x) = \ln \dfrac{x}{2}$

$f(x) = -14 \cos \pi x$

$f(x) = -14 \sin \pi x$

CONSTRUCTED RESPONSE

4. Determine the minimum values of the quadratic function $f(x) = x^2 - 4x - 1$ and a cosine function whose graph has an amplitude of 4.5 and the *x*-axis as its midline. Which function has the lesser minimum value?

_____

_____

5. Let $f(x) = 5 \cos \pi x$, and let $g(x)$ be the function represented by the graph.

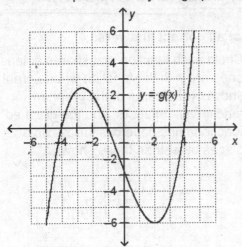

a. Which function has a lesser minimum value on the interval $-4 \le x \le 4$? Explain.

_____

b. Which function has a greater maximum value on the interval $-4 \le x \le 4$? Explain.

_____

6. The population of city A was 12,831 in 1900 and grew 5% per year for the next 10 years. For the same period, the function $P(t) = 11,572(1.07)^t$ models the population of city B, where P is the population and t is the time, in years since 1900.

a. What was the population of each city in 1900? Which city had the greater population?

_____

b. At what annual rate was the population of each city increasing over this period? The population of which city was growing faster?

_____

c. What was the population of each city in 1910? Which city had the greater population?

_____

d. During which year were the populations of the two cities equal? (Use a graphing utility to answer this question.)

_____

7. Two masses m_1 and m_2 are each suspended from a spring. Each spring is compressed a certain distance, and the mass begins oscillating about its equilibrium position once released. The function $d_1(t) = 4 \cos \frac{\pi}{4} t$ gives the displacement d_1, in centimeters, of mass m_1 at time t, in seconds since the mass begins oscillating. The table shows the displacement d_2, in centimeters, of mass m_2 at time t, in seconds since the mass begins oscillating.

t	d_2
0	6
2	4.2
4	0
6	-4.2
8	-6
10	-4.2
12	0
14	4.2
16	6

a. The spring attached to which of the two masses was compressed farther initially? Explain.

_____

_____

b. Which of the two masses is oscillating faster? Explain.

_____

_____

The student will determine an explicit expression, a recursive process, or steps for calculation from a context.

SELECTED RESPONSE
Select the correct answer.

1. Circle the function that makes a true statement.

   Moore's law proposes that the number of transistors on integrated circuits doubles approximately every 2 years. The function that models the number N of transistors on integrated circuits t years after $N = 68,000$ is

$N(t) = 68,000(2t)$
$N(t) = 68,000(2)^t$
$N(t) = 68,000(2)^{0.5t}$
$N(t) = 2t + 68,000$

2. The members of a model rocket club launch their latest creation. The rocket shoots to an altitude of 225 feet, reaching a vertical velocity of 130 feet per second, before running out of fuel. Recall that acceleration due to gravity is -32 feet per second per second. What equation models the height h, in feet, of the rocket t seconds after running out of fuel?

   (A) $h(t) = 16t^2 + 130t + 225$

   (B) $h(t) = -16t^2 - 130t + 225$

   (C) $h(t) = 16t^2 + 130t - 225$

   (D) $h(t) = -16t^2 + 130t + 225$

3. A customer has a $100 gift card to a local coffee shop. Suppose the customer, using the card, spends $5 per day at the shop. Which recursive rule represents the card's remaining balance B, in dollars, after using the card for t days?

   (A) $B(0) = 100$ and $B(t) = B(t-1) - 5$ for $1 \le t \le 20$

   (B) $B(0) = 95$ and $B(t) = B(t-1) - 5$ for $1 \le t \le 20$

   (C) $B(1) = 100$ and $B(t+1) = B(t) - 5$ for $1 \le t \le 20$

   (D) $B(1) = 95$ and $B(t+1) = B(t) - 5$ for $2 \le t \le 20$

Select all correct answers.

4. Engineering students at a university develop protective packaging for an egg that is dropped from the roof of a building. The velocity of the falling egg increases by 32 feet per second each second. Which functions model the relationship between the egg's velocity v, in feet per second, and the amount of time t, in seconds, that the egg has fallen?

   (A) $v(t) = 32t$

   (B) $v(t) = 32^t$

   (C) $v(t) = t + 32$

   (D) $v(0) = 0$ and $v(t+1) = v(t) + 32$ for $t \ge 0$

   (E) $v(0) = 32$ and $v(t+1) = v(t) + 32$ for $t \ge 0$

   (F) $v(0) = 0$ and $v(t) = v(t-1) + 32$ for $t \ge 1$

CONSTRUCTED RESPONSE

5. The ends of a piece of string are tied together to form a loop 200 inches long. Find the area A, in square inches, of a rectangle formed by stretching the string tight and forming a quadrilateral with four right angles as a function of the width w, in inches, of the rectangle.

   _____

   _____

6. A small company manufactures racing bicycles. On average, each bicycle requires $575 of materials and $375 of labor to produce. The company also has average weekly fixed costs of $1295 (for insurance, utilities, and other expenses not tied to materials or labor). Write a function to model the daily cost C, in dollars, of producing b bicycles per day.

   _____

   _____

7. The value of a lottery prize doubles each week until there is a winner. If the prize is $1000 the first week, write a recursive function rule and an explicit function rule to model the value of the prize P, in dollars, after t weeks without a winner.

_____

_____

8. A rancher plans to use 1800 meters of fencing to make three holding pens by enclosing a rectangular region and dividing it into three smaller rectangular regions of equal area, as shown.

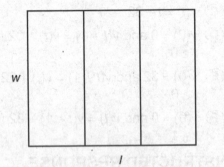

a. Find a function for the area A, in square meters, of each smaller rectangular region as a function of the width w, in meters.

_____

b. What is the maximum value of $A(w)$?

_____

c. State the domain and range of $A(w)$ for this situation.

_____

9. The monthly payment for a $100,000 mortgage with an annual interest rate of 3% for 15 years is $690.58. Interest is compounded monthly, and a payment is due after the interest for a month has accrued.

a. Describe the steps needed to calculate the total amount, in dollars, owed on the mortgage after making each monthly payment. Be as specific as possible.

_____

_____

_____

_____

_____

_____

_____

_____

_____

_____

b. Write a recursive function for the balance B, in dollars, owed after making p monthly payments.

_____

_____

The student will combine standard function types using arithmetic operations.

SELECTED RESPONSE
Select the correct answer.

1. Circle the function that makes a true statement.

   The cost C, in dollars, of producing n items can be modeled by the function $C(n) = an + b$, where a is the cost to produce each item and b is the fixed cost. The function that models the per-item cost of producing n items

   is
   $$\boxed{\begin{array}{l} C_{PI}(n) = a + \dfrac{b}{n} \\[2mm] C_{PI}(n) = \dfrac{a+b}{n} \\[2mm] C_{PI}(n) = a + b \\[2mm] C_{PI}(n) = an + \dfrac{b}{n} \end{array}}$$.

Select all correct answers.

2. The functions $L(x) = 3x + 5$, $W(x) = 2x + 1$, and $H(x) = 2x$ give the length, width, and height, respectively, in centimeters, of a right rectangular pyramid. Which combinations of these functions are correct?

   Ⓐ $P(x) = 10x + 10$ represents the perimeter P, in centimeters, of the base.

   Ⓑ $P(x) = 10x + 12$ represents the perimeter P, in centimeters, of the base.

   Ⓒ $A(x) = 6x^2 + 13x + 5$ represents the area A, in square centimeters, of the base.

   Ⓓ $A(x) = 6x^2 + 10x$ represents the area A, in square centimeters, of the base.

   Ⓔ $V(x) = 4x^3 + \dfrac{26}{3}x^2 + \dfrac{10}{3}x$ represents the volume V, in cubic centimeters, of the pyramid.

   Ⓕ $V(x) = 12x^3 + 26x^2 + 10x$ represents the volume V, in cubic centimeters, of the pyramid.

CONSTRUCTED RESPONSE

3. A landscape architect is designing a rectangular reflecting pool. The exact dimensions of the pool have yet to be determined, but the pool's length will be 3 times its width, and the pool's depth will be 6 inches. The bottom and sides of the pool will be lined with glass tiles that cost $3.75 per square foot. Write functions to represent the areas, in square feet, of the bottom and of each pair of sides of the pool. Then write a function to represent the total area, in square feet, to be tiled. Finally, use this area function to write a function that relates the cost of tiling the pool to the pool's width. Be sure to define all variables.

   _____

   _____

4. Three neighboring towns share a high school. The functions $N_A(t) = 341(1.055)^t$, $N_B(t) = 227(1.051)^t$, and $N_C(t) = 112(1.059)^t$ model the number N of high school students from towns A, B, and C, respectively, t years after the year 2000. Write a function to model the fraction of the students at the high school from town B at time t.

5. A right rectangular prism has edge lengths of $x + 1$ inches, $x + 2$ inches, and $x + 3$ inches, for $x \geq 0$. Another right rectangular prism has edge lengths of $x + 2$ inches, $x + 3$ inches, and $x + 4$ inches over the same domain. Write functions of x that model the volumes, in cubic inches, of each rectangular solid. Then determine the function of x that models the positive difference, in cubic inches, between the two volumes.

   _____

   _____

6. Marcelle has several investments. At the moment, she has $1250 in a certificate of deposit that earns 3% annual interest compounded monthly, $1000 in a money market account that averages 6% annual interest compounded quarterly, and $5000 in a retirement fund that has an average annual return of 7%, which is compounded annually. Assuming these investments continue to perform at the current rates, write a function for the total amount A, in dollars, in Marcelle's investments as a function of time t, in years.

_____

_____

7. Now that Yousef is retired, he farms as a hobby. He sells his produce at a weekly local farmers' market. This week, Yousef is harvesting tomatoes. He pays local students $2 per case to pick the tomatoes and has about $175 in weekly fixed costs for fuel, packaging, and other expenses.

   a. Write a function for the total costs C, in dollars, for this week as a function of the number n of cases of tomatoes picked.

   _____

   b. Assuming Yousef sells all of his tomatoes for $27 per case, write a function for the revenue R, in dollars, for this week as a function of n.

   _____

   c. Use the functions found in parts a and b to write a function for the profit P, in dollars, for this week as a function of n.

   _____

   d. How many cases does Yousef need to sell to break even?

   _____

8. A carnival ride consists of two wheels attached at the ends of a long bar whose midpoint is supported by a tower, as shown. When the ride is in motion, each wheel rotates counterclockwise once every 5 seconds as the bar rotates counterclockwise once every 12 seconds. The bar is 50 feet long, the diameter of the wheels is 30 feet, and the tower is 45 feet tall. Suppose a rider is seated at point A when the ride begins.

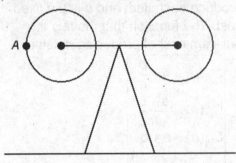

   a. Write a function to model the height, in feet, of the center of the wheel that contains the rider t seconds after the ride begins.

   _____

   b. Write another function to model the height, in feet, of the rider relative to the center of the wheel that contains the rider t seconds after the ride begins.

   _____

   c. Write a third function to model the height, in feet, of the rider relative to the ground t seconds after the ride begins

   _____

The student will write arithmetic and geometric sequences both recursively and explicitly, and use them to model.

SELECTED RESPONSE
Select the correct answer.

1. A theater has 18 rows of seats. There are 22 seats in the first row, 26 seats in the second row, 30 seats in the third row, and so on. Which of the following is a recursive formula for the arithmetic sequence that represents this situation?

   (A) $f(0) = 18$, $f(n) = f(n-1) + 4$
   for $1 \leq n \leq 18$

   (B) $f(1) = 22$, $f(n) = f(n-1) + 4$
   for $2 \leq n \leq 18$

   (C) $f(n) = 18 + 4n$

   (D) $f(n) = 22 + 4(n-1)$

2. The table below shows the balance b, in dollars, of Daryl's savings account t years after he made an initial deposit. What is an explicit formula for the geometric sequence that represents this situation?

Time, t (years)	Balance, b (dollars)
1	$1218
2	$1236.27
3	$1254.81
4	$1273.64

   (A) $b(t) = 1.015(1218)^{t-1}$

   (B) $b(t) = 1218(1.015)^{t}$

   (C) $b(t) = 1218 + 1.015(t-1)$

   (D) $b(t) = 1218(1.015)^{t-1}$

Select all correct answers.

3. Amelia earns $36,000 in the first year from her new job and earns a 6% raise each year. Circle each function that models Amelia's pay p, in dollars, in year t of her job.

   $p(0) = 36{,}000$, $p(t) = 1.06 \cdot p(t-1)$
   for $t \geq 1$

   $p(1) = 36{,}000$, $p(t) = 1.06 \cdot p(t-1)$
   for $t \geq 2$

   $p(t) = 36{,}000 \cdot 1.06^{t-1}$ for $t \geq 1$

   $p(t) = 1.06 \cdot 36{,}000^{t-1}$ for $t \geq 1$

   $p(t) = 1.06(t-1) + 36{,}000$ for $t \geq 1$

   $p(t) = 38{,}160 \cdot 1.06^{t-2}$ for $t \geq 1$

CONSTRUCTED RESPONSE

4. Calvin is practicing the trumpet for an audition to play in a band. He starts practicing the trumpet 40 minutes the first day and then increases his practice time by 5 minutes per day. The audition is on the 10th day.

   a. Write a recursive rule that represents the time t, in minutes, Calvin practices on day d.

   _____

   b. Write an explicit rule that represents the time t, in minutes, Calvin practices on day d.

   _____

   c. Use the result from part b to find how long Calvin practices on the 8th day. Show your work.

   _____

   _____

   _____

Name _____ Date _____ Class _____

5. The table displays the speed of a car s, in feet per second, t seconds after it starts coasting.

Time, t (seconds)	Speed, s (ft/sec)
1	57
2	54.15
3	51.44
4	48.87

a. Explain why this sequence is geometric.

_____

_____

_____

_____

_____

b. Write an explicit rule for this sequence using the values from the table.

_____

_____

c. Use the result from part b to write a recursive rule for this sequence.

_____

_____

d. What is the speed of the car when it begins to coast? Show your work.

_____

_____

_____

_____

_____

6. The table below shows the cost c, in dollars, of a private party on a boat based on the number of people p attending.

People, p	Cost, c (dollars)
2	306
3	334
4	362
5	390

a. Does an arithmetic sequence or a geometric sequence model this situation? Justify your answer by using the values in the table.

_____

_____

_____

_____

_____

_____

_____

b. Write an explicit formula and a recursive formula for the sequence. Show your work.

_____

_____

_____

_____

c. How much would it cost for 44 people to attend the private party? Show your work.

_____

_____

_____

_____

_____

_____

Name _____ Date _____ Class_____

The student will identify the effect of a transformation on the graph of *f*(*x*) and write an equation of a transformed graph.

SELECTED RESPONSE

Select the correct answer.

1. How do you transform the graph of

   $f(x) = \dfrac{1}{x}$ to obtain the graph of

   $g(x) = \dfrac{8}{x+5} - 7$?

   A) Shift left 5 units, horizontally stretch by a factor of 8, and shift down 7 units.

   B) Shift left 5 units, vertically stretch by a factor of 8, and shift down 7 units.

   C) Shift right 5 units, vertically stretch by a factor of 8, and shift down 7 units.

   D) Shift left 7 units, vertically stretch by a factor of 8, and shift up 5 units.

Select all correct answers.

2. The graph of *g*(*x*) is shown. Circle each of the transformations that could have been performed to obtain the graph of *g*(*x*) from the graph of $f(x) = \sqrt[3]{x}$.

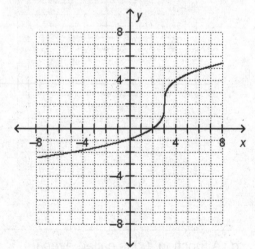

   A shift to the right by 2 units

   A shift to the right by 3 units

   A vertical stretch by a factor of 2

   A vertical shrink by a factor of $\dfrac{1}{4}$

   A shift up by 3 units

   A shift up by 2 units

CONSTRUCTED RESPONSE

3. The graph of *g*(*x*) is shown. Describe the transformations used to obtain the graph of *g*(*x*) from the graph of its parent function $f(x) = x^3$, and write a rule for *g*(*x*).

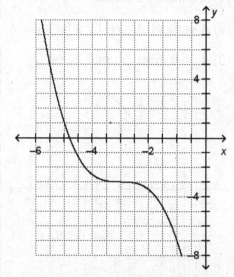

_____

_____

4. The graph of *g*(*x*) is shown. Describe the transformations used to obtain the graph of *g*(*x*) from the graph of its parent function $f(x) = 3^x$, and write a rule for *g*(*x*).

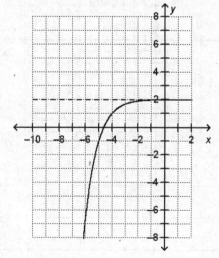

_____

_____

5. Carlos incorrectly graphed the function $g(x) = -4 \log_2 (x - 2) + 3$ using transformations of the graph of $f(x) = \log_2 x$. First, he stated what transformations to perform. Then, he drew the graph. Analyze and correct his work.

(1) A shift left 2 units

(2) A vertical stretch by a factor of 4

(3) A shift down 3 units

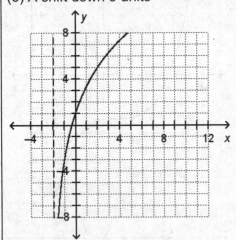

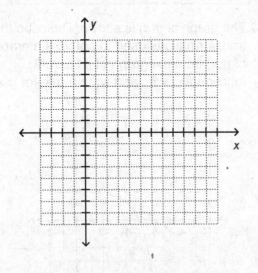

_____

_____

_____

_____

6. a. Graph $f(x) = \sin x$ and $g(x) = \sin (-x)$ on the same coordinate plane. State what transformation you used to obtain the graph of $g(x)$ from the graph of $f(x)$.

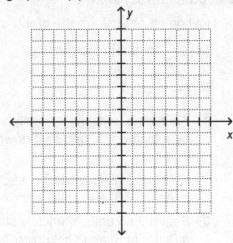

b. Graph $p(x) = \cos x$ and $q(x) = \cos (-x)$ on the same coordinate plane. State what transformation you used to obtain the graph of $q(x)$ from the graph of $p(x)$.

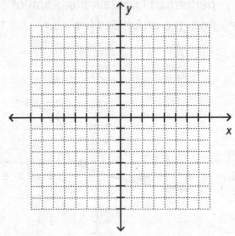

c. A function $f(x)$ is called *even* if $f(-x) = f(x)$ for all values of x. A function $f(x)$ is called *odd* if $f(-x) = -f(x)$ for all values of x. Use the graphs from parts a and b to determine whether the parent sine and cosine functions are even, odd, or neither. Explain your reasoning.

The student will solve $f(x) = c$ for a simple function f that has an inverse and write an expression for the inverse.

SELECTED RESPONSE

Select the correct answer.

1. What is $f^{-1}(x)$ if $f(x) = \dfrac{x+2}{x-3}$, $x \neq 3$?

   Ⓐ $f^{-1}(x) = \dfrac{x+2}{x-3}$, $x \neq 3$

   Ⓑ $f^{-1}(x) = \dfrac{3x+2}{x-1}$, $x \neq 1$

   Ⓒ $f^{-1}(x) = \dfrac{x-1}{3x+2}$, $x \neq -\dfrac{2}{3}$

   Ⓓ $f^{-1}(x) = \dfrac{x-3}{x+2}$, $x \neq -2$

2. Circle the function that makes a true statement. The inverse of
$$f(x) = 2\ln\left(\dfrac{x}{3}\right) + 5$$

is
$$\boxed{\begin{aligned} f^{-1}(x) &= e^{2\ln\left(\frac{x}{3}\right)+5} \\[4pt] f^{-1}(x) &= e^{\frac{3x-15}{2}} \\[4pt] f^{-1}(x) &= 3e^{\frac{x-5}{2}} \\[4pt] f^{-1}(x) &= 3e^{\frac{x}{2}-5} \end{aligned}}$$

Select all correct answers.

3. Which functions are equivalent forms of the inverse of $f(x) = \dfrac{2x-5}{x-3}$, $x \neq 3$?

   Ⓐ $f^{-1}(x) = \dfrac{3x-5}{x+2}$, $x \neq -2$

   Ⓑ $f^{-1}(x) = \dfrac{3x-5}{x-2}$, $x \neq 2$

   Ⓒ $f^{-1}(x) = \dfrac{3x+5}{x-2}$, $x \neq 2$

   Ⓓ $f^{-1}(x) = 3 + \dfrac{1}{x-2}$, $x \neq 2$

   Ⓔ $f^{-1}(x) = 3 + \dfrac{1}{x+2}$, $x \neq -2$

   Ⓕ $f^{-1}(x) = 3 - \dfrac{1}{x+2}$, $x \neq -2$

CONSTRUCTED RESPONSE

4. Find the inverse of $f(x) = \dfrac{1}{2}\sqrt[3]{x+4} - 5$. Show your work.

   _____

   _____

   _____

   _____

   _____

5. Find the inverse of $f(x) = \sqrt{x-2}$. Show your work. Also, describe how the domain and range of $f(x)$ compare to the domain and range of its inverse. What are the domain and range of the inverse?

   _____

   _____

   _____

   _____

   _____

   _____

6. Let $f(x) = \dfrac{4x+3}{x-9}$.

   a. Find the domain and range of $f(x)$.

   _____

   _____

   b. Find the inverse of $f(x)$.

   _____

   c. Find the domain and range of the inverse function.

   _____

7. Let $f(x) = 15(4)^{x-2} + 7$. Find the inverse of $f(x)$ and use it to find x such that $f(x) = 247$. Show your work.

_____

_____

_____

_____

_____

_____

_____

_____

8. The function $p(t) = 1000(2)^t$ models the population p of a bacteria colony at time t, in weeks after the initial population was observed. Write a function that expresses time t as a function of population p. Use this function to find how many weeks it takes the population to grow to 32,000. Verify your result with $p(t)$. Show all work.

_____

_____

_____

_____

_____

_____

_____

_____

9. The function $p(d) = \sqrt{d^3}$ models the orbital period p, in years, of a planet as a function of its distance d, in astronomical units, from the Sun. An astronomical unit is a unit of distance that is equal to the distance between Earth and the Sun.

a. Find the inverse of $p(d)$. Show your work.

_____

_____

_____

_____

_____

b. What does the inverse function model?

_____

_____

c. To the nearest 0.1 astronomical unit, how far is Jupiter from the Sun if its orbital period is about 11.86 years? Show your work.

_____

_____

_____

_____

_____

_____

Name _____ Date _____ Class_____

The student will express as a logarithm the solution to $ab^{ct} = d$, if the base b is 2, 10, or e, and evaluate the logarithm.

SELECTED RESPONSE

Select the correct answer.

1. The half-life of carbon-14 is about 5730 years. The amount A, in grams, of carbon-14 remaining in a sample of A_0 grams after time t, in years, is modeled by $A = A_0 \cdot 2^{-\frac{t}{5730}}$. What is an equivalent equation solved for t?

   Ⓐ $t = \dfrac{\log_2 \frac{A_0}{A}}{5730}$

   Ⓑ $t = -5730 \log_2 \dfrac{A_0}{A}$

   Ⓒ $t = \dfrac{\log_2 \frac{A}{A_0}}{5730}$

   Ⓓ $t = -5730 \log_2 \dfrac{A}{A_0}$

2. Circle the time that makes a true statement.

   The exact time t, in years, needed for the balance of an account that earns 2% annual interest compounded continuously to double, assuming no deposits other than the initial deposit and no withdrawals

   is $\boxed{\begin{array}{l} t = \dfrac{\ln 2}{0.02} \text{ years} \\[2mm] t = \dfrac{\log 2}{0.02} \text{ years} \\[2mm] t = 50 \text{ years} \\[2mm] t = \dfrac{e^{0.02}}{0.02} \text{ years} \end{array}}$.

Select all correct answers.

3. In the equation $ab^{ct} = d$, a, b, c, and d are positive real numbers, and t is a variable. Which of the following are solutions of the equation?

   Ⓐ $t = \dfrac{\ln \frac{d}{a}}{\ln c}$

   Ⓓ $t = \dfrac{\log_b \frac{d}{a}}{\log_b c}$

   Ⓑ $t = \dfrac{\log \frac{d}{a}}{c \log b}$

   Ⓔ $t = \dfrac{\log_b \frac{d}{a}}{c}$

   Ⓒ $t = \dfrac{\ln \frac{d}{a}}{c \ln b}$

   Ⓕ $t = \dfrac{\log \frac{d}{a}}{c}$

CONSTRUCTED RESPONSE

4. The number N of bacteria in a culture is modeled by the function $N(t) = 500(2)^{0.5t}$, where t is the time in hours. After how many hours will the population reach 1,000,000 bacteria? Give an exact answer in terms of logarithms as well as the answer rounded to the nearest hour. Show your work.

   _____

   _____

5. The pH of a substance is a measure of the acidity or alkalinity of the substance. The pH is related to the concentration of hydrogen ions [H⁺], in moles per liter, by the equation $10^{-pH} = [H^+]$. What is the pH, to the nearest tenth, of a substance if $[H^+] = 0.00005$ mole per liter?

   _____

   _____

© Houghton Mifflin Harcourt Publishing Company

Getting Ready for High-Stakes Assessment   87   Algebra 2

6. A customer at a restaurant orders a cup of tea, so the waiter places a tea bag into a room temperature mug, pours in boiling water, and lets the mug sit while the tea steeps and cools. The function $T(t) = 72 + 140e^{-0.14t}$ models the temperature T, in degrees Fahrenheit, of the tea as a function of the time t, in minutes. For safety reasons, the waiter does not want to serve the tea until its temperature is no more than 125 °F. How long should the waiter allow the mug of tea to sit before serving? To be safe, round up to the nearest minute.

_____

_____

7. Identify and correct the error that a student made when solving the equation $7(10)^{0.25x} = 5375$.

$$7(10)^{0.25x} = 5375$$
$$10^{0.25x} = \frac{5375}{7}$$
$$\log 10^{0.25x} = \log \frac{5375}{7}$$
$$0.25x \log 10 = \log \frac{5375}{7}$$
$$0.25x = \log 5375 - \log 7$$
$$0.25x = \log 5368$$
$$x = 4 \log 5368$$
$$x \approx 14.92$$

_____

_____

8. Marcus deposits $500 in an account that earns 3% annual interest compounded continuously. Assume there are no other deposits and no withdrawals.

a. After how many years would the account balance triple? Give an exact answer in terms of logarithmic expressions as well as the answer rounded to the nearest tenth of a year. Show your work.

_____

_____

b. If Marcus wants the account balance to triple in 20 years, what annual interest rate would an account earning interest compounded continuously need to have? Give an exact answer in terms of logarithmic expressions as well as the answer rounded to the nearest tenth of a percent. Show your work.

_____

_____

9. An industrial accident floods a room with radon-222, a radioactive gas. The employees evacuate immediately and seal the room. Monitoring equipment reports that the radioactivity level in the room is 844 picoCuries per liter. The half-life of radon-222 is about 3.8 days. Write a function to model the radioactivity level L, in picoCuries, in the room as a function of the time t, in days. After how many days is the radioactivity level below the recommended maximum level of 4 picoCuries per liter? To be safe, round up to the nearest day.

_____

_____

The student will interpret the parameters in a linear or exponential function in terms of a context.

SELECTED RESPONSE
Select the correct answer.

1. The function $P(t) = 50(2)^{0.25t}$ models the population P of a certain type of bacteria after t hours. How long does it take the initial population to double?

   Ⓐ 0.25 hour

   Ⓑ 2 hours

   Ⓒ 4 hours

   Ⓓ 50 hours

2. Shen is interested in joining a health and fitness club. There are four clubs in his area. The functions $C_1(t) = 25t + 50$, $C_2(t) = 30t + 25$, $C_3(t) = 50t$, and $C_4(t) = 35t + 10$ model the cost C, in dollars, of being a member for time t, in months, at each of the four clubs. Which club charges the greatest joining fee?

   Ⓐ Club 1 with cost $C_1(t)$

   Ⓑ Club 2 with cost $C_2(t)$

   Ⓒ Club 3 with cost $C_3(t)$

   Ⓓ Club 4 with cost $C_4(t)$

3. The function $GDP(t) = 0.504(1.18)^t$ models the gross domestic product GDP, in trillions of dollars, as a function of the time t, in years, of a nation from 2002 to 2011. What is the annual percentage increase in the gross domestic product during this period?

   Ⓐ 0.18%

   Ⓑ 0.504%

   Ⓒ 1.18%

   Ⓓ 18%

Select all correct answers.

4. The function $A(t) = 850(1.0025)^{12t}$ models the amount A, in dollars, at time t, in years, in a bank account that earns interest compounded periodically. Circle each statement about this account that is true.

   The initial amount is $850.00.

   The initial amount is $875.85.

   The interest is compounded quarterly.

   The interest is compounded monthly.

   The interest is compounded yearly.

   The account earns 0.25% annual interest.

   The account earns 2.50% annual interest.

   The account earns 3.00% annual interest.

CONSTRUCTED RESPONSE

5. The function $C(t) = 1.25t + 8.5$ models the total cost C, in dollars, for a large cheese pizza with t toppings from a local restaurant. How much does a large plain cheese pizza from this restaurant cost?

   _____

6. The function $A(t) = 500e^{0.03t}$ models the amount A, in dollars, at time t, in years, in a bank account that earns interest compounded continuously. What annual interest rate does the account earn?

   _____

7. Salama plans to open a savings account at one of two banks. The function $A_1(t) = 425(1.00625)^{4t}$ models the amount A_1, in dollars, at time t, in years, in an account at the first bank. The function $A_2(t) = 425(1.00175)^{12t}$ models the amount A_2, in dollars, at time t, in years, in an account at the second bank. What is the effective annual rate for an account at each bank? Which bank offers the account with the higher effective annual rate?

_____

_____

8. The function $A(t) = 750(0.7937)^t$ models the amount A, in grams, remaining in a sample of fermium-253 after t days.

   a. What is the initial amount of fermium-253 in the sample? Explain.

   _____

   _____

   b. Interpret the value 0.7937 in the function.

   _____

   _____

   c. To the nearest day, what is the half-life of fermium-253? Explain.

   _____

   _____

9. A car traveling along a long straight highway at a constant speed passes a rest area. The distance d, in miles, the car must travel to reach the next rest area as a function of the time t, in hours, is modeled by $d(t) = 100 - 65t$.

   a. At what speed is the car traveling? Explain.

   _____

   _____

   b. What is the distance between the two rest areas? Explain.

   _____

   _____

Name _____ Date _____ Class _____

The student will understand radian measure as the length of the arc on the unit circle subtended by an angle.

SELECTED RESPONSE
Select the correct answer.

1. Circle the angle measure that makes a true statement.

   An arc on the unit circle is $\frac{3\pi}{4}$ units long.

   The radian measure of the arc's central

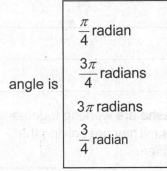

   angle is
   - $\frac{\pi}{4}$ radian
   - $\frac{3\pi}{4}$ radians
   - 3π radians
   - $\frac{3}{4}$ radian

2. An arc on the unit circle is $\frac{4\pi}{3}$ units long. What is the degree measure of the arc's central angle?
   - (A) 60°
   - (B) 120°
   - (C) 240°
   - (D) 300°

3. On the unit circle, a central angle θ in standard position intercepts an arc that is 2 units long. If you reflect angle θ across the y-axis to create a new angle α in standard position, what is the measure of α?
   - (A) $2 - 2\pi$ radians
   - (B) $2 - \pi$ radians
   - (C) $\pi - 2$ radians
   - (D) $2\pi - 2$ radians

Select all correct answers.

4. Which arc lengths on the unit circle have central angles with measures less than 180°?
   - (A) $\frac{\pi}{2}$
   - (E) $\frac{3\pi}{2}$
   - (B) $\frac{11\pi}{6}$
   - (F) $\frac{5\pi}{6}$
   - (C) $\frac{3\pi}{4}$
   - (G) $\frac{\pi}{6}$
   - (D) $\frac{5\pi}{3}$
   - (H) 2π

CONSTRUCTED RESPONSE

5. Explain why the radian measure of an angle is the length of the arc that it intercepts on the unit circle.

   _____
   _____
   _____

6. The central angle θ in a circle of radius 8 intercepts an arc of length 10π. If the same central angle intercepts an arc on the unit circle, what is the length of that arc? Explain.

   _____
   _____

7. The following figure shows an arc of length 1 on the unit circle. The measure of the arc's central angle θ is therefore 1 radian. Use the figure to find the measures of α and β. (The length of each given arc is a whole number.)

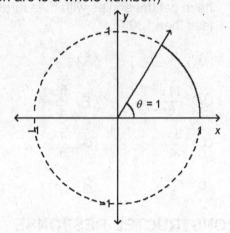

a.

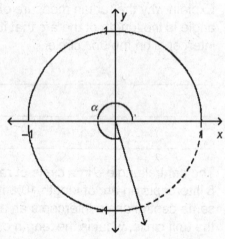

b.

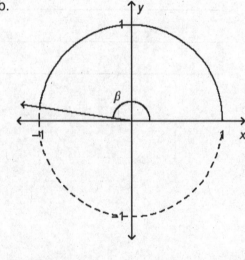

8. The arc intercepted by a certain central angle on the unit circle has a length of $\frac{11\pi}{6}$ units. Find the lengths of the arcs intercepted by the same angle on circles of radius 2 units, 3 units, and 4 units. Explain and show your work.

_____

_____

_____

_____

_____

9. Dean and Sasha are working together on an assignment. They are solving the following problem.

> The arc intercepted by a central angle α on a circle of radius 10 units is 15π units. Find the length of the arc intercepted by a central angle θ on the unit circle given that the measure of θ is half the measure of α.

Dean says the length of the arc intercepted by θ on the unit circle is $\frac{3\pi}{2}$ units, whereas Sasha says this length is $\frac{3\pi}{4}$ units. Which answer should they use? Explain and show your work.

_____

_____

_____

_____

_____

Name _____ Date _____ Class _____

The student will explain how the unit circle in the coordinate plane enables the extension of trigonometric functions.

SELECTED RESPONSE
Select the correct answer.

1. How do you find the value of sin θ for a given value of θ $(0 \le \theta < 2\pi)$ using the unit circle?

   (A) The angle of rotation θ in standard position traverses an arc on the unit circle. The x-coordinate of the arc's endpoint that lies on the terminal side of θ is the value of sin θ.

   (B) The angle of rotation θ in standard position traverses an arc on the unit circle. The y-coordinate of the arc's endpoint that lies on the terminal side of θ is the value of sin θ.

   (C) The angle of rotation θ in standard position traverses an arc on the unit circle. The ratio of the x-coordinate to the y-coordinate of the arc's endpoint that lies on the terminal side of θ is the value of sin θ.

   (D) The angle of rotation θ in standard position traverses an arc on the unit circle. The ratio of the y-coordinate to the x-coordinate of the arc's endpoint that lies on the terminal side of θ is the value of sin θ.

2. Which of the following always has the same value as sin θ?

   (A) $\sin\left(\theta + \dfrac{\pi}{2}\right)$

   (B) $\sin(\theta + \pi)$

   (C) $\sin\left(\theta + \dfrac{3\pi}{2}\right)$

   (D) $\sin(\theta + 2\pi)$

Select all correct answers.

3. Circle each angle that has the same trigonometric values as $\theta = \dfrac{3\pi}{4}$.

   $\alpha = \dfrac{11\pi}{4}$ $\alpha = -\dfrac{5\pi}{4}$

   $\alpha = \dfrac{63\pi}{4}$ $\alpha = \dfrac{35\pi}{4}$

   $\alpha = -\dfrac{25\pi}{4}$ $\alpha = -\dfrac{9\pi}{4}$

CONSTRUCTED RESPONSE

4. Describe how to find the values of the following trigonometric expressions using the unit circle. Then, find the values.

   a. sin π

   _____

   _____

   b. cos $\dfrac{4\pi}{3}$

   _____

   _____

   c. tan $\dfrac{2\pi}{3}$

   _____

   _____

5. Describe how to find the values of the following trigonometric expressions using the unit circle. Then, find the values.

   a. sin $\dfrac{14\pi}{3}$

   _____

   _____

   b. cos $\dfrac{59\pi}{6}$

   _____

   _____

6. Describe how to find the values of the following trigonometric expressions using the unit circle. Then, find the values.

   a. $\tan\left(-\dfrac{19\pi}{3}\right)$

   _____

   _____

   b. $\sin\left(-\dfrac{3\pi}{4}\right)$

   _____

   _____

7. On the graph shown, the points A, B, C, D, E, F, and G mark off arc lengths of 1 unit counterclockwise from A to G along the unit circle. Use the graph to estimate the following trigonometric function values to the nearest tenth.

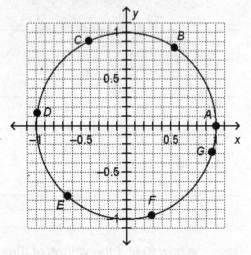

   a. $\sin 1$

   _____

   b. $\cos 6$

   _____

   c. $\tan 2$

   _____

   d. $\tan 5.5$

   _____

8. A student evaluates $\cos\dfrac{19\pi}{6}$ by repeatedly subtracting π from the angle until the result is between 0 and π, as shown. Explain why this is incorrect, and find the correct value.

$$
\begin{aligned}
\cos\frac{19\pi}{6} &= \cos\frac{13\pi}{6} \\
&= \cos\frac{7\pi}{6} \\
&= \cos\frac{\pi}{6} \\
&= \frac{\sqrt{3}}{2}
\end{aligned}
$$

   _____

   _____

   _____

9. Explain how the unit circle can be used to find $\sin\theta$, $\cos\theta$, and $\tan\theta$ for any central angle θ (positive or negative). What are the values of these functions in general?

   _____

   _____

   _____

   _____

   _____

Name _____ Date _____ Class_____

The student will choose trigonometric functions to model periodic phenomena.

SELECTED RESPONSE

Select the correct answer.

1. A mass is suspended from a cable to form a pendulum. When the mass is displaced from its resting position and allowed to swing, the displacement of the mass relative to its resting position is periodic. What is the general form of a trigonometric function with amplitude a and frequency b that could model the displacement d of the mass relative to its resting position as a function of the time t after passing through the resting position?

   Ⓐ $d(t) = a \cos 2\pi bt$

   Ⓑ $d(t) = a \cos bt$

   Ⓒ $d(t) = a \sin bt$

   Ⓓ $d(t) = a \sin 2\pi bt$

2. A mass is suspended from a spring. When the mass is displaced vertically from its resting position and released, the displacement of the mass relative to its resting position is periodic. If the mass is raised 2 inches from its resting position and released, which function could model the displacement d, in inches, of the mass t seconds after being released? (Assume that the displacement above the resting position is positive and the displacement below the resting position is negative.)

   Ⓐ $d(t) = 2 \sin t$

   Ⓑ $d(t) = 2 \cos t$

   Ⓒ $d(t) = -2 \sin t$

   Ⓓ $d(t) = -2 \cos t$

Match each description with the correct function.

Using the list of general forms of trigonometric functions of displacement d at time t at the bottom of the page, write the form that models the description of periodic motion.

3. The motion starts at the minimum value and repeats every b time units.

4. The motion starts at the minimum value and repeats every $\dfrac{1}{b}$ time units.

5. The motion increases to a maximum from the midline value and repeats every b time units.

6. The motion starts at the maximum value and repeats every $\dfrac{1}{b}$ time units.

7. The motion increases to a maximum from the midline value and repeats every $\dfrac{1}{b}$ time units.

8. The motion decreases to a minimum from the midline value and repeats every b time units.

$d(t) = a \cos \dfrac{2\pi t}{b} + k$	$d(t) = a \cos 2b\pi t + k$	$d(t) = -a \cos \dfrac{2\pi t}{b} + k$	$d(t) = -a \cos 2b\pi t + k$
$d(t) = a \sin \dfrac{2\pi t}{b} + k$	$d(t) = a \sin 2b\pi t + k$	$d(t) = -a \sin \dfrac{2\pi t}{b} + k$	$d(t) = -a \sin 2b\pi t + k$

Select all correct answers.

9. As a bicycle travels at a steady rate, the distance between a reflector attached to the spokes of the front wheel and the ground varies between 3.5 inches and 25.5 inches 8 times per second. Which functions model the distance d, in inches, between the reflector and the ground at time t, in seconds?

Ⓐ $d(t) = 25.5 - 11 \sin \dfrac{\pi t}{8}$

Ⓑ $d(t) = 14.5 - 11 \sin 8\pi t$

Ⓒ $d(t) = 14.5 - 11 \cos 8\pi(t + 3.5)$

Ⓓ $d(t) = 14.5 - 11 \sin \dfrac{\pi t}{8}$

Ⓔ $d(t) = 3.5 + 11 \cos 8\pi t$

Ⓕ $d(t) = 14.5 + 11 \sin 8\pi t$

Ⓖ $d(t) = 3.5 + 11 \sin 8\pi(t + 25.5)$

Ⓗ $d(t) = 14.5 + 11 \cos \dfrac{\pi t}{8}$

CONSTRUCTED RESPONSE

10. One of the world's tallest Ferris wheels sits on a building 15 meters high and has a radius of 75 meters. It completes 1 revolution every 30 minutes. Mike wrote the function $h_1(t) = 75 \sin \dfrac{\pi}{15}(t - 7.5) + 90$ to model the height h of a passenger t minutes after getting on the Ferris wheel. Lupe thinks the height is given by the function

$h_2(t) = 75 \cos \dfrac{\pi}{15}(t - 15) + 90.$

a. Explain why both are correct.

_____

_____

b. What does this say about using sine and cosine to model periodic phenomena? Explain. (Hint: Think about transformations.)

_____

_____

11. The *stroke* is the distance the pistons in an engine move inside the cylinders. Suppose the stroke for a particular engine is 9.3 centimeters and the engine is idling at 750 revolutions per minute. Write a function to model the height h, in centimeters, of the top of a piston relative to its lowest position in the cylinder at time t, in seconds, after passing through the lowest position.

_____

12. The object of a carnival game is to use a water pistol to hit as many targets as possible in 1 minute. There are three spinning discs that face the player. On the edge of each disc are four evenly-spaced targets. Only the very top of each disc is visible to the player, so only one target on each disc can be visible at any moment. The disc on the left (L) completes 1 rotation every 2 seconds, the disc in the middle (M) completes 1 revolution every 3 seconds, and the disc on the right (R) completes 1 rotation every 4 seconds.

a. When the game begins, a target is visible on each disc. Model the periodic appearance a of the targets on each disc as a function of the time t, in seconds, since the game begins.

_____

_____

b. The pistol shoots a 0.1 second pulse of water when the trigger is pulled, and it needs 0.3 second to recharge after each shot. The pulse of water takes 0.2 second to reach a disc. If a player shoots at a target 7.8 seconds after the game begins but misses the target, what is the next target the player can try to hit? When should the player shoot to hit this target? Explain your reasoning.

_____

_____

The student will prove the Pythagorean identity $\sin^2(\theta) + \cos^2(\theta) = 1$ and use it to find $\sin(\theta)$, $\cos(\theta)$, or $\tan(\theta)$.

SELECTED RESPONSE

Select the correct answer.

1. Circle the number that makes a true statement.

   Given that $\sin \theta = 0.3817$ and $\frac{\pi}{2} < \theta < \pi$,

   the approximate value of $\cos \theta$

   is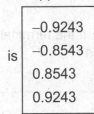
−0.9243
−0.8543
0.8543
0.9243

2. Given that $\cos \theta = 0.7087$ and $\frac{3\pi}{2} < \theta < 2\pi$, what is the approximate value of $\sin \theta$?

   Ⓐ −0.7055

   Ⓑ −0.4977

   Ⓒ 0.4977

   Ⓓ 0.7055

3. Given that $\tan \theta = 3.0096$ and $0 < \theta < \frac{\pi}{2}$, what is the approximate value of $\cos \theta$?

   Ⓐ −0.3153

   Ⓑ −0.0994

   Ⓒ 0.0994

   Ⓓ 0.3153

Select all correct answers.

4. Given that $\sin \theta = -0.2794$, which of the following statements can be true?

   Ⓐ $\cos \theta \approx 0.9602$ where $0 < \theta < \frac{\pi}{2}$

   Ⓑ $\cos \theta \approx -0.9602$ where $\frac{\pi}{2} < \theta < \pi$

   Ⓒ $\cos \theta \approx -0.9602$ where $\pi < \theta < \frac{3\pi}{2}$

   Ⓓ $\cos \theta \approx 0.9602$ where $\frac{3\pi}{2} < \theta < 2\pi$

   Ⓔ $\tan \theta \approx 0.2910$ where $0 < \theta < \frac{\pi}{2}$

   Ⓕ $\tan \theta \approx -0.2910$ where $\frac{\pi}{2} < \theta < \pi$

   Ⓖ $\tan \theta \approx 0.2910$ where $\pi < \theta < \frac{3\pi}{2}$

   Ⓗ $\tan \theta \approx -0.2910$ where $\frac{3\pi}{2} < \theta < 2\pi$

CONSTRUCTED RESPONSE

5. Use the unit circle definitions of sine, cosine, and tangent to complete parts a–c.

   a. Write $\tan \theta$ in terms of $\sin \theta$ and $\cos \theta$. Explain your reasoning.

   _____

   _____

   b. Use the identity from part a to write $\sin \theta$ in terms of $\tan \theta$ and $\cos \theta$.

   _____

   c. Use the identity from part a to write $\cos \theta$ in terms of $\tan \theta$ and $\sin \theta$.

   _____

6. Given that $\cos \theta = -0.7702$ and $\dfrac{\pi}{2} < \theta < \pi$, determine the signs of $\sin \theta$ and $\tan \theta$. Then, find the approximate values of $\sin \theta$ and $\tan \theta$.

_____

_____

7. Given that $\tan \theta = 3.2603$ and $\pi < \theta < \dfrac{3\pi}{2}$, Simon incorrectly found that $\cos \theta \approx 0.2932$ and $\sin \theta \approx 0.9560$. His work is shown below. Explain and correct his error(s).

> Since $\sin \theta = \tan \theta \cos \theta$,
> $\sin \theta = 3.2603 \cos \theta$.
> $$\sin^2 \theta + \cos^2 \theta = 1$$
> $$(3.2603 \cos \theta)^2 + \cos^2 \theta = 1$$
> $$10.629556 \cos^2 \theta + \cos^2 \theta \approx 1$$
> $$11.629556 \cos^2 \theta \approx 1$$
> $$\cos^2 \theta \approx 0.085988$$
> $$\cos \theta \approx \sqrt{0.085988}$$
> $$\cos \theta \approx 0.293237$$
> $$\sin \theta \approx (3.2603)(0.293237) \approx 0.956041$$

_____

_____

_____

_____

8. Use the unit circle definitions of sine and cosine to prove the Pythagorean identity $\sin^2 \theta + \cos^2 \theta = 1$.

_____

_____

_____

_____

9. Suppose $\tan \theta = 0.6966$.

a. In what quadrants can the terminal side of θ fall? Explain.

_____

_____

b. Find the possible approximate values of $\sin \theta$. Show your work.

_____

_____

_____

_____

c. For each approximate value of $\sin \theta$ in part b, find the corresponding approximate value of $\cos \theta$. Show your work.

_____

_____

_____

Name _____ Date _____ Class_____

The student will derive the equation of a parabola given a focus and directrix.

SELECTED RESPONSE
Select the correct answer.

1. In the diagram below, F is the focus of the parabola, line d is the directrix, and $\overline{QP} \perp d$. What is the relationship between FP and QP?

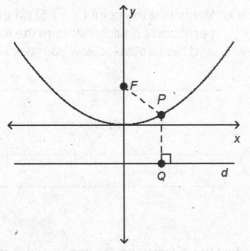

   Ⓐ $FP < QP$

   Ⓑ $FP = QP$

   Ⓒ $FP > QP$

   Ⓓ A relationship cannot be determined.

2. Which point is always on a parabola with focus $F(0, p)$ and directrix $y = -p$?

   Ⓐ $(0, 0)$

   Ⓑ $(0, p)$

   Ⓒ $(p, 0)$

   Ⓓ (p, p)

3. Which focus and directrix correspond to a parabola described by $y = \dfrac{1}{16}x^2$?

   Ⓐ Focus $(0, -4)$ and directrix $y = -4$

   Ⓑ Focus $(0, 4)$ and directrix $y = 4$

   Ⓒ Focus $(0, -4)$ and directrix $y = 4$

   Ⓓ Focus $(0, 4)$ and directrix $y = -4$

Select all correct answers.

4. Circle the points that are on the parabola with focus $(0, 4)$ and directrix $y = -4$.

   $(-8, 4)$ $(4, 1)$

   $(0, -4)$ $(9, 12)$

   $(0, 4)$ $(12, 9)$

CONSTRUCTED RESPONSE

5. Use the distance formula to write the equation of the parabola with focus $F(0, -3)$ and directrix $y = 3$. Show your work.

   _____

   _____

6. A parabola has focus $(0, -2)$ and directrix $y = 2$.

   a. Write the equation of the parabola.

   _____

   b. Graph the parabola, the focus, and the directrix below.

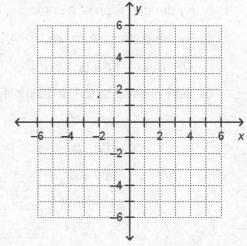

   c. Use the graph from part b to find the vertex of the parabola. Explain your answer.

   _____

   _____

7. Eric is writing the equation of a parabola with focus $F(0, 7)$ and directrix $y = -7$. His work, including a mistake, is shown below. What is Eric's mistake? What is the correct equation of the parabola?

$$\sqrt{(x-0)^2 + (y-7)^2} = \sqrt{(x-x)^2 + (y+7)^2}$$
$$\sqrt{x^2 + (y-7)^2} = \sqrt{(y+7)^2}$$
$$\sqrt{x^2 + (y-7)^2} = |y+7|$$
$$x^2 + (y-7)^2 = |y+7|^2$$
$$x^2 + y^2 + 49 = y^2 + 14y + 49$$
$$x^2 = 14y$$
$$\frac{1}{14}x^2 = y$$

_____

_____

8. The focus of a parabola whose vertex is at the origin is the point $(0, -1.5)$.

a. What is the directrix of the parabola?

_____

b. What is the equation of the parabola?

_____

_____

c. Verify that the point $(3, -1.5)$ on the parabola is equidistant from the focus and the directrix. Show your work.

_____

_____

_____

_____

9. Let the focus of a parabola be the point $F(0, p)$ and let the directrix be the line $y = -p$. Let $P(x, y)$ be a point on the parabola. Complete the work below to derive the equation of the parabola.

a. Let Q be the point of intersection of the perpendicular from P and the directrix. The coordinates of Q are _____.

b. By the definition of a parabola, $FP =$ _____.

c. By the distance formula, $FP = \sqrt{(x-0)^2 + (y-p)^2} = \sqrt{x^2 + (y-p)^2}$ and

$QP = \sqrt{(x-x)^2 + [y-(-p)]^2} = \sqrt{0 + (y+p)^2} =$ _____.

d. Set FP equal to QP and simplify.

$$\sqrt{x^2 + (y-p)^2} = |y+p|$$

$$x^2 + (y-p)^2 = |y+p|^2 \qquad \text{Square both sides.}$$

$$x^2 + y^2 - 2py + p^2 = \rule{3cm}{0.4pt} \qquad \text{Expand the squared terms.}$$

$$x^2 - 2py = \rule{3cm}{0.4pt} \qquad \text{Subtract } y^2 \text{ and } p^2 \text{ from both sides.}$$

$$x^2 = \rule{3cm}{0.4pt} \qquad \text{Add } 2py \text{ to both sides.}$$

$$\rule{3cm}{0.4pt} = y \qquad \text{Solve for } y.$$

Name _____ Date _____ Class_____

The student will use mean and standard deviation to fit data to a normal distribution and to estimate percentages.

For items that ask you to use the standard normal distribution, refer to the standard normal table on the next page.

SELECTED RESPONSE
Select the correct answer.

1. The scores for the mathematics portion of a standardized test are normally distributed with a mean of 514 points and a standard deviation of 117 points. What is the probability that a randomly selected student has a score of 610 points or less on the test? Use the standard normal distribution to estimate the probability.

  Ⓐ 29.4%   Ⓒ 79.4%

  Ⓑ 20.6%   Ⓓ 68%

2. If the mean of a data set is 20, the standard deviation is 1.5, and the distribution of the data values is approximately normal, about 95% of the data values fall in what interval centered on the mean?

  Ⓐ 18.5 to 21.5 Ⓒ 15.5 to 24.5

  Ⓑ 17 to 23   Ⓓ 14 to 26

Select all correct answers.

3. Which of the following data sets are NOT likely to be normally distributed?

  Ⓐ The day of the month on which randomly selected students were born

  Ⓑ The final exam scores of all students taking the same class and given the same final exam in a large school district

  Ⓒ The number of wheels on the next 100 vehicles that pass by a point along a highway

  Ⓓ The heights of tenth-grade male students at a large high school

  Ⓔ The IQs of the students at a large high school

Match each mass with the correct percent.

Using the list of percents on the right, write the approximate percent of the data values that fall within the given interval if a data set consisting of the weights of 50 jars of honey has a mean weight of 435 grams with a standard deviation of 2.5 grams. The data distribution is approximately normal.

4. 432.5 g to 435 g   `[_____]`

5. 427.5 g to 442.5 g   `[_____]`

6. 432.5 g to 437.5 g   `[_____]`

7. 430 g to 440 g   `[_____]`

8. Greater than 440 g   `[_____]`

9. Less than 435 g   `[_____]`

2.5%
16%
34%
50%
68%
84%
95%
99.7%

CONSTRUCTED RESPONSE

10. The IQ scores of the students at a school are normally distributed with a mean of 100 points and a standard deviation of 15 points. Use the standard normal distribution to estimate each percent.

  a. The percent of students with an IQ score below 80 points

  _____

  b. The percent of students with an IQ score below 127 points

  _____

11. The wing lengths of houseflies are normally distributed with a mean of 45.5 mm and a standard deviation of 3.92 mm. Use the standard normal distribution to estimate each percent.

  a. The percent of houseflies with wing lengths over 35 millimeters

  _____

  b. The percent of houseflies with wing lengths over 50 millimeters

  _____

© Houghton Mifflin Harcourt Publishing Company

12. The grapefruits harvested at a large orchard have a mean mass of 482 grams with a standard deviation of 31 grams. Assuming that the masses of these grapefruits are approximately normally distributed, Jess uses the 68-95-99.7 rule to estimate the percent of grapefruits that have masses between 451 grams and 544 grams. Jess incorrectly reasons that since 451 grams is 2 standard deviations below the mean and 544 is 2 standard deviations above the mean, 95% of the grapefruits have masses between 451 grams and 544 grams. Identify his error and determine the correct estimate.

_____

_____

_____

_____

13. The heights of the male students at Bart's school are normally distributed with a mean of 68 inches and a standard deviation of 2 inches.

a. What percent of the male students at Bart's school are more than 68 inches tall? Explain.

_____

_____

b. What percent of the male students at Bart's school are less than 64 inches tall? Explain. (Hint: Use the 68-95-99.7 rule.)

_____

_____

14. The scores on a recent district-wide math test are normally distributed with a mean of 82 points and a standard deviation of 5 points. Use the standard normal distribution to answer each question.

a. What percent of students scored between 70 and 75 on the test? Show your work.

_____

_____

b. What percent of students scored at least 90 on the test? Show your work.

_____

_____

c. What percent of students scored at most 65 on the test? Show your work.

_____

_____

Standard Normal Table

z	.0	.1	.2	.3	.4	.5	.6	.7	.8	.9
−3	.0013	.0010	.0007	.0005	.0003	.0002	.0002	.0001	.0001	.0000+
−2	.0228	.0179	.0139	.0107	.0082	.0062	.0047	.0035	.0026	.0019
−1	.1587	.1357	.1151	.0968	.0808	.0668	.0548	.0446	.0359	.0287
−0	.5000	.4602	.4207	.3821	.3446	.3085	.2743	.2420	.2119	.1841
0	.5000	.5398	.5793	.6179	.6554	.6915	.7257	.7580	.7881	.8159
1	.8413	.8643	.8849	.9032	.9192	.9332	.9452	.9554	.9641	.9713
2	.9772	.9821	.9861	.9893	.9918	.9938	.9953	.9965	.9974	.9981
3	.9987	.9990	.9993	.9995	.9997	.9998	.9998	.9999	.9999	1.000−

(Note: In the table, ".0000+" means slightly more than 0 and "1.000−" means slightly less than 1.)

The student will understand statistics as a process for making inferences based on a random sample.

SELECTED RESPONSE
Select the correct answer.

1. Aimee and Stan work in the same department for a large corporation. They are curious about the proportion of their coworkers who have children. Aimee obtains a list of all the workers in the department, randomly picks 20 names from the list, and asks those coworkers if they have children. She finds that 72% of those surveyed have children. Stan waits in the break room one morning and asks the first 20 coworkers that pass by if they have children. He finds that 85% of those surveyed have children. Which result is the better estimate of the proportion of coworkers who have children?

   Ⓐ 72%

   Ⓑ 85%

   Ⓒ Both results are equally good estimates.

   Ⓓ Neither result is a good estimate.

2. For a science project, two students need to estimate the average height of the 273 students in the senior class at their school. Each student measures the heights of 20 randomly selected members of the senior class. The mean height for one sample is 166 cm, and the mean height for the other sample is 170 cm. Which is the better estimate of the mean height of the students in the senior class?

   Ⓐ 166 cm

   Ⓑ 170 cm

   Ⓒ Both results are equally good estimates.

   Ⓓ Neither result is a good estimate.

3. The junior class at a high school plans to sell T-shirts featuring the school mascot, Billy the goat. To estimate how many of each size T-shirt to order, the class president and vice president each survey a random sample of the students at the school to see if the students are interested in buying a T-shirt and what size or sizes each would buy. The class president surveys 40 students and finds that about 75% are interested in buying T-shirts, and of these students, 30% would buy a medium, 50% would buy a large, and 20% would buy an extra large. The class vice president surveys 20 students and finds that about 85% are interested in buying T-shirts, and of these students, 25% would buy a medium, 60% would buy a large, and 15% would buy an extra large. What is the best estimate of the percentage of the T-shirts ordered that should be extra large?

   Ⓐ 15%   Ⓒ 75%

   Ⓑ 20%   Ⓓ 85%

Select all correct answers.

4. The entertainment committee for a retirement community surveys a random sample of the residents. Each resident in the sample is asked his or her age, gender, and favorite type of movie (comedy, drama, adventure, and so on). Circle the parameters that the committee can make inferences from using the data from the survey.

   The mean age of the residents

   The mean income of the residents

   The mean age of retired people

   The proportion of the residents who prefer dramas

   The proportion of retired people who are male

   The proportion of the residents over 75 years of age

Name _____ Date _____ Class_____

CONSTRUCTED RESPONSE

5. Veata wants to know what percent of students at her school are left-hand dominant. She knows that among her group of friends, 4 of the 7 are left-hand dominant. Veata recalls that when students were randomly assigned to groups to clean the school grounds for Earth day, she was the only student in the group of 8 that was left-hand dominant. She also notices that 7 of the 28 students in her art class are left-hand dominant. Explain which sample Veata should use to determine the best estimate for the percent of students at the school who are left-hand dominant. What is this best estimate?

_____

_____

6. To estimate his revenue from the sale of his calves, a rancher weighs a random sample of 30 calves. Can the rancher use the mean weight from this sample to estimate the mean weight of all 872 calves in his herd? Explain.

_____

_____

7. A candidate for public office is planning a campaign stop in a small city. Before arriving, the candidate wants to know if the majority of the city's registered voters support her or her opponent. The candidate reviews the results from two recent polls. One poll found that 271 of 500 randomly selected registered voters support the candidate. The other found that 144 of 300 randomly selected registered voters support the candidate. Should the candidate expect to meet more registered voters who support her or her opponent while in the city? Explain.

_____

_____

8. Three concerned citizens—Arturo, Bernice, and Chu—each collect data about the average speed at which cars travel through their neighborhood for one 5-day workweek. The posted speed limit is 30 mph.

Arturo observes the first 10 cars he sees pass his house each morning for the week as he prepares to go to work, and records the time it takes each car to cover the distance between two signs. The mean of the corresponding speeds for the 50 cars observed is 32 mph.

Each day, Bernice randomly selects 4 locations in the neighborhood and 4 times between 6 a.m. and 6 p.m. At each selected time, Bernice goes to the corresponding selected location and notes the distance between two fixed objects. She records the time the first car that passes takes to travel the distance between the objects. The mean of the corresponding speeds for the 20 cars observed is 30 mph.

At random times throughout the day, Chu drives around the neighborhood, follows cars he believes are speeding, and records his speed. The mean speed for the 38 cars Chu follows for the week is 47 mph.

Evaluate the sampling method used by each concerned citizen. Include how likely each sample is to be representative of all the cars that pass through the neighborhood. Which is the best estimate of the average speed?

_____

_____

_____

_____

_____

_____

The student will decide if a specified model is consistent with results from a given data-generating process.

SELECTED RESPONSE
Select the correct answer.

1. A probability model claims that $P(A) = 0.82$ and $P(B) = 0.18$. Which result is most unlikely if the model is correct?

   Ⓐ *A* occurs 15 times, and *B* occurs 25 times in 40 trials.

   Ⓑ *A* occurs 50 times, and *B* occurs 10 times in 60 trials.

   Ⓒ *A* occurs 70 times, and *B* occurs 20 times in 90 trials.

   Ⓓ *A* occurs 85 times, and *B* occurs 15 times in 100 trials.

2. Circle the result that makes a true statement.

   A probability model for a spinner with 4 unequal sections labeled 1, 2, 3, and 4 is shown. The result that is most unlikely for this model is:

The spinner lands on 1 twice in 20 spins.
The spinner lands on 2 twice in 5 spins.
The spinner lands on 3 twice in 25 spins.
The spinner lands on 4 twice in 10 spins.

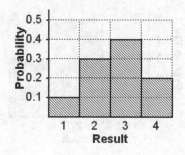

Select all correct answers.

3. The spinner shown has 3 equal sections. If you spin the spinner 90 times, which of these outcomes are very unlikely?

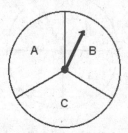

   Ⓐ The spinner lands on A 30 times.

   Ⓑ The spinner lands on B 5 times.

   Ⓒ The spinner lands on C 0 times.

   Ⓓ The spinner lands on A 70 times.

   Ⓔ The spinner lands on B 25 times.

   Ⓕ The spinner lands on C 1 time.

CONSTRUCTED RESPONSE

4. If you roll a fair number cube with numbers 1 through 6 on it, the probability that you roll a certain number is $\frac{1}{6}$.

   Would you question whether a number cube was fair if you rolled a 2 four times in a row? Explain.

   _____

   _____

5. A probability model claims that $P(A) = 0.2$, $P(B) = 0.3$, and $P(C) = 0.5$. The dot plot shows the results of 10 trials. Describe the likelihood of these results for the given model.

   _____

   _____

6. The spinner shown has 4 equal sections, so the probabilities that the spinner lands on any given number are equal. Ronaldo spins the spinner twice and records the sum of the two numbers on which the spinner lands.

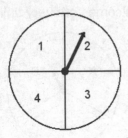

a. Complete the table to show the probability model for the sum of the two numbers.

Sum	Probability
2	
3	
4	
5	
6	
7	
8	

b. Make a histogram of the probability model. Be sure to show the scale on the vertical axis.

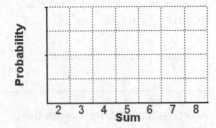

c. Ronaldo records the sums for 20 pairs of spins. The dot plot shows the results. Is the model consistent with these results? Explain.

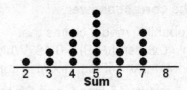

_____

_____

7. To win a board game, Jean needs to roll a 4 on a number cube, which has the numbers 1 through 6 on it. After how many rolls without rolling a 4 should Jean conclude the number cube is not fair? Complete the table for the probability of not rolling a 4 n times for various values of n, and use the probabilities to support your answer.

n	5	10	15	20	25
P(not a 4)					

_____

8. A probability distribution for a spinner with 10 equal sections labeled 1, 2, or 3 is shown. Suppose you spin the spinner four times. What is the probability that the spinner lands on 1 each time? On 2 each time? On 3 each time? Which of these results would make you question whether the model is correct? Explain.

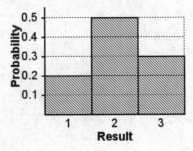

_____

_____

Name _____ Date _____ Class_____

The student will recognize the purposes of and differences among surveys, experiments, and observational studies.

SELECTED RESPONSE
Select the correct answer.

1. Which of these scientific studies of cholesterol is a survey?

   (A) Researchers compare the cholesterol levels of people with heart disease to the cholesterol levels of people with healthy hearts.

   (B) Researchers raise one group of rats on a high cholesterol diet and another group on a low cholesterol diet. The researchers record the incidence of heart disease in each group.

   (C) Researchers measure the cholesterol levels of randomly selected people with heart disease.

   (D) Researchers record the incidence of heart disease in people with high cholesterol levels and people with normal cholesterol levels.

2. Which of these scientific studies of brain function is an observational study?

   (A) Researchers record the times subjects need to solve a puzzle.

   (B) Researchers record the times subjects need to solve similar puzzles near sea level and at an altitude of 6000 feet with and without supplemental oxygen.

   (C) Researchers record the times subjects need to solve similar puzzles near sea level and at an altitude of 6000 feet.

   (D) Researchers record the times subjects near sea level need to solve a puzzle and the times 100 subjects at an altitude of 6000 feet need to solve the same puzzle.

3. Which of these scientific studies of two cold remedies is an experiment?

   (A) Researchers give cold remedy A or cold remedy B to people with colds, and then observe the duration of the cold symptoms exhibited by each group.

   (B) Researchers observe the cold symptoms exhibited by people with colds who choose to take cold remedy A and people with colds who choose to take cold remedy B.

   (C) Researchers ask people with colds if they feel better after taking cold remedy A or cold remedy B.

   (D) Researchers include questionnaires in packages of cold remedy A and cold remedy B for the users to complete while taking the remedy and then return to the researchers.

Select all correct answers.

4. Circle each true statement.

   Experiments can establish cause and effect.

   Observational studies create conditions by imposing treatments.

   Surveys compare characteristics of interest about a population.

   Randomization reduces the influence of confounding variables.

   Observational studies, unlike experiments, involve only existing conditions.

   Surveys do not involve randomization.

CONSTRUCTED RESPONSE

5. Describe the main purposes of surveys, observational studies, and experiments as they relate to characteristics of interest in a population.

_____

6. For study A, researchers select two schools in a district and convince the administrators to have the teachers follow the traditional method to teach math at one school and a new method at the other. For study B, researchers randomly select one fourth-grade class in a school district that follows the traditional method to teach math and one fourth-grade class in another school district that follows the new method. Which of these studies is an observational study, and which is an experiment? Explain how you know.

_____

7. Explain how surveys, observational studies, and experiments can include randomization and describe the effects of randomization.

_____

_____

8. To determine if there is a relationship between the hours of light per day and the number of eggs hens lay, researchers place 100 hens in each of two windowless coops, one of which is lighted for 10 hours per day and the other for 16 hours per day. The researchers record the number of eggs laid by the hens in each coop.

    a. Identify the characteristic of interest for the research study.

    _____

    b. Is this research study an observational study or an experiment? Explain.

    _____

    c. If this research study is an observational study, identify the factor (the existing condition). If the research study is an experiment, identify the treatment imposed to create the condition.

    _____

d. Describe a way the researchers could include randomization in this study, and explain the effects of this randomization.

_____

e. Could the results of this study be used to establish a cause-and-effect relationship between the hours of light per day and the number of eggs chickens lay? Explain.

_____

9. To determine if there is a relationship between exposure to asbestos and lung cancer, researchers record the incidence of lung cancer in 1000 people who were exposed to asbestos and 1000 people who were never exposed to asbestos.

    a. Identify the characteristic of interest for the research study.

    _____

    b. Is this research study an observational study or an experiment? Explain.

    _____

    c. If this research study is an observational study, identify the factor (the existing condition). If the research study is an experiment, identify the treatment imposed to create the condition.

    _____

    d. Describe a way the researchers could include randomization in this study, and explain the effects of this randomization.

    _____

    e. Could the results of this study be used to establish a cause-and-effect relationship between exposure to asbestos and lung cancer? Explain.

    _____

The student will use data from a survey to estimate a population mean or proportion, and find a margin of error.

SELECTED RESPONSE
Select the correct answer.

1. For samples of 100 from a population having proportion p, the graph shows the reasonably likely values of the sample proportion $\hat{p}$ (those that fall within 2 standard deviations of p). For instance, when $p = 0.06$ (read from the vertical axis), the horizontal bar shows that the reasonably likely values of $\hat{p}$ fall between 0.01 and 0.12 (read from the horizontal axis). For what range of population proportions would a sample proportion of 10% be reasonably likely for a sample of 100?

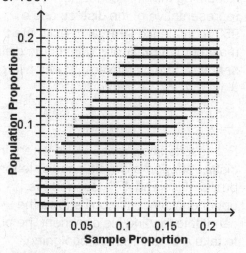

Sample Proportion

Ⓐ 0.04 to 0.16   Ⓒ 0.01 to 0.05

Ⓑ 0.06 to 0.17   Ⓓ 0 to 0.03

2. When using a $c\%$ confidence interval to estimate a population mean or proportion, how does the interval change as the value of c changes?

  Ⓐ The interval gets wider as the value of c increases.

  Ⓑ The interval gets narrower as the value of c increases.

  Ⓒ The interval depends on the sample mean or proportion, not the value of c.

  Ⓓ The interval depends on the sample standard deviation, not the value of c.

Select all correct answers.

3. Circle the intervals that are possible confidence interval estimates of a population mean given a sample mean of 42.8 feet and some confidence level. (Assume that the population standard deviation is known and that the sample size is fixed.)

37.8 feet to 47.8 feet

39.3 feet to 46.3 feet

40.0 feet to 45.0 feet

40.0 feet to 45.6 feet

40.3 feet to 44.3 feet

41.0 feet to 44.6 feet

CONSTRUCTED RESPONSE

4. A survey of a random sample of 1000 registered voters finds that 417 voters plan to vote for a particular state proposition. Estimate the proportion of registered voters in the state who plan to vote for the proposition using an interval with a margin of error of 2 standard deviations. Round percents to the nearest tenth.

_____

5. To estimate the percent of people in her town who are left-hand dominant, Suzi surveys a random sample of 25 residents and finds that 4 are left-hand dominant. Use the fact that $z_{0.95} = 1.96$ to form a 95% confidence interval estimate of the proportion of people in Suzi's town who are left-hand dominant. Round numbers to the nearest thousandth.

_____

6. Suppose 60% of a population supports a ballot question. The table shows the frequency of the sample proportions $\hat{p}$ that result from 100 simulations of sampling 50 members of a population with proportion $p = 0.6$. Notice that an interval centered on the population proportion plus or minus 0.03 (that is, from $0.6 - 0.03 = 0.57$ to $0.6 + 0.03 = 0.603$) contains $11 + 13 + 11 = 35$ of the 100 sample proportions. This means that the margin of error for a confidence interval of 35% is ±3%.

Interval	Frequency
$0.43 \leq x < 0.45$	1
$0.45 \leq x < 0.47$	1
$0.47 \leq x < 0.49$	2
$0.49 \leq x < 0.51$	5
$0.51 \leq x < 0.53$	6
$0.53 \leq x < 0.55$	8
$0.55 \leq x < 0.57$	9
$0.57 \leq x < 0.59$	11
$0.59 \leq x < 0.61$	13
$0.61 \leq x < 0.63$	11
$0.63 \leq x < 0.65$	10
$0.65 \leq x < 0.67$	9
$0.67 \leq x < 0.69$	5
$0.69 \leq x < 0.71$	3
$0.71 \leq x < 0.73$	2
$0.73 \leq x < 0.75$	1
$0.75 \leq x < 0.77$	1
$0.77 \leq x < 0.79$	1
$0.79 \leq x < 0.81$	0
$0.81 \leq x < 0.83$	1

a. What confidence interval corresponds to a margin of error of ±7%?

_____

b. What is the margin of error for a 90% confidence interval?

_____

7. A farmer finds the mean mass for a random sample of 200 eggs laid by his hens to be 57.2 grams. If the masses of eggs for this breed of hen are normally distributed with standard deviation 1.5 grams, estimate the mean mass, to the nearest tenth of a gram, of the eggs for this breed using a 99% confidence interval. Note that $z_{0.99} = 2.576$.

_____

8. A school district serves about 19,000 students in 28 schools. The superintendent of the district receives a report from the principal of one of the schools that of the 200 students from that school moving on to middle school, 2 have severe peanut allergies. Assuming that this school is representative of the district, use a 95% confidence interval to estimate the maximum number of students the district serves who have severe peanut allergies. Note that $z_{0.95} = 1.96$.

_____

9. Poll results show that 53% of voters in a district support a certain candidate for public office and 47% support his opponent. Since the poll shows the candidate leading his opponent, he plans to take a break from campaigning.

a. Use the fact that the poll surveyed 300 voters in the district to construct 95% confidence intervals for the proportion of voters in the district who support each candidate. Note that $z_{0.95} = 1.96$.

_____

b. Is the candidate wise to take a break? Use the intervals from part a to explain why or why not.

_____

_____

The student will use an experiment to compare treatments, and use simulation to decide if differences are significant.

SELECTED RESPONSE
Select the correct answer.

1. Circle the result that makes a true statement. An experiment to determine if a treatment for insomnia increases a person's average number of hours of sleep per night is performed on 200 people who report they have difficulty sleeping. Researchers randomly assign 100 people to the treatment group and 100 people to the control group. After the study, the researchers determined that 24 of the subjects in the treatment group and 14 of the subjects in the control group average more sleep per night. The data from the two groups are resampled 150 times, and the table shows the distribution of the differences of the proportions for the reconfigured treatment and control groups. (Note that resampling involves randomly scrambling the data from the treatment and control groups and calculating a difference of proportions for the reconfigured groups: treatment group proportion minus control group proportion. Each new difference obtained from a resampling becomes part of a resampling distribution.) The percent of the differences that are less than the difference obtained from the experiment's

results is
| 2% |
| 6% |
| 94% |
| 98% |
.

Difference	Frequency
−0.14	3
−0.10	9
−0.06	24
−0.02	40
0.02	39
0.06	26
0.10	6
0.14	3

2. Researchers randomly select 10 students who are given breakfast and 10 students who are not. Each group takes an 80 question math test 1 hour after the students in the treatment group eat breakfast, and the researchers record the number of questions each student answers correctly. The data are shown in the table. Resampling the data finds that 95% of the differences of the means for the reconfigured treatment and control groups are less than 5.2. (Note that resampling involves randomly scrambling the data from the treatment and control groups and calculating a difference of means for the reconfigured groups: treatment group mean minus control group mean. Each new difference obtained from a resampling becomes part of a resampling distribution.) Is there evidence that eating breakfast increases performance on the math test?

Number of correct questions	
Breakfast	**No breakfast**
56	58
62	54
68	62
73	48
56	68
57	65
49	60
72	72
62	52
57	45

A Yes; the difference of the means from the experiment is greater than 5.2.

B Yes; the difference of the means from the experiment is less than 5.2.

C No; the difference of the means from the experiment is greater than 5.2.

D No; the difference of the means from the experiment is less than 5.2.

Name _____ Date _____ Class_____

CONSTRUCTED RESPONSE

3. A recreational baseball player wants to know if he can hit balls farther using a new type of bat. The player uses a pitching machine to throw consistent easy pitches and hits 10 balls with the new type of bat while an assistant measures the distance the ball travels to the nearest foot. The player then hits 10 balls using a standard bat while the assistant measures the distances. The data are shown in the table below. Resampling the data finds that 95% of the differences of the means for the reconfigured treatment and control groups are less than 10.5 feet. (Note that resampling involves randomly scrambling the data from the treatment and control groups and calculating a difference of means for the reconfigured groups: treatment group mean minus control group mean. Each new difference obtained from a resampling becomes part of a resampling distribution.) Is there evidence the player can hit balls farther using the new type of bat? Show your work.

Distance (feet)	
New type of bat	**Standard bat**
328	348
347	327
337	314
345	302
363	320
352	343
331	324
329	317
346	315
327	335

_____

_____

_____

4. To test the effectiveness of a new product designed to prevent crabgrass from invading lawns, researchers divide a lawn into 10 plots with equal area, 5 of which are randomly selected and treated with the new product. After 3 months, the researchers count the number of crabgrass plants growing in each plot. The results are shown in the table. The data are resampled 100 times, and the histogram shows the distribution of the differences of the means for the reconfigured treatment and control groups. (Note that resampling involves randomly scrambling the data from the treatment and control groups and calculating a difference of means for the reconfigured groups: treatment group mean minus control group mean. Each new difference obtained from a resampling becomes part of a resampling distribution.) Does the experiment provide evidence that the new product prevents crabgrass from invading lawns? Use the resampling distribution to justify your answer.

Plot	Number of crabgrass plants
Treated	3, 7, 0, 4, 1
Untreated	6, 7, 8, 7, 6

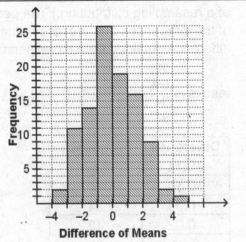

_____

_____

The student will evaluate reports based on data.

SELECTED RESPONSE
Select the correct answer.

1. Researchers measured the levels of fluoride in young children and gave tests to measure their intellectual development over several years. The results show that young children with higher exposure to fluoride tend to have lower IQ scores later in life. What can the researchers claim based on these results?

   Ⓐ There is a relationship between fluoride levels in children and IQ scores.

   Ⓑ Exposure to higher levels of fluoride reduces IQ.

   Ⓒ There is no relationship between fluoride levels in children and IQ scores.

   Ⓓ Reducing exposure to fluoride can increase IQ.

2. To determine if a new drug reduces blood pressure, researchers randomly select 800 people with high blood pressure, and the subjects are randomly assigned to the control group or the treatment group. The subjects in the control group take a placebo daily for 30 days, while those in the treatment group take the new drug daily for 30 days. The results show that the mean blood pressure for the control group is unchanged, while the mean blood pressure for the treatment group is significantly lower. What can the researchers claim based on these results?

   Ⓐ There is no relationship between the new drug and blood pressure.

   Ⓑ There is a relationship between the new drug and blood pressure, but causation cannot be determined.

   Ⓒ Taking the new drug reduces blood pressure.

   Ⓓ Not taking the new drug increases blood pressure.

Select all correct answers.

3. Researchers randomly select 100 people with heart disease and 100 people with healthy hearts and have the subjects complete a questionnaire about their diets. The results show that on average, the subjects with heart disease eat more red meat than the subjects with healthy hearts. Circle each of the following that could be a confounding variable that produces the observed effect.

   The subjects with healthy hearts may exercise regularly, which prevents the disease.

   The subjects with heart disease may smoke cigarettes, and that is the cause of the disease.

   The subjects with healthy hearts may eat some type of food, such as fish, that prevents the disease.

   The subjects with heart disease may salt red meat heavily, and the salt could cause the disease.

   The subjects with healthy hearts may be genetically predisposed not to develop heart disease.

   The subjects with heart disease may be genetically predisposed to develop heart disease.

CONSTRUCTED RESPONSE

4. Researchers randomly select 10,000 subjects. The researchers measure the blood cholesterol level of each subject and check for signs of heart disease annually for 30 years.

   a. Describe results that would support a claim that high blood cholesterol level is related to heart disease.

   _____

   b. Describe results that would support a claim that high blood cholesterol causes heart disease.

   _____

5. To determine if vibration syndrome, a loss of feeling in the hands, is related to occupational exposure to vibration, researchers studied workers at two foundries and a shipyard. Workers who had never used vibrating hand tools comprised the control group. Workers in the exposed groups were in the same work locations as the control workers and used vibrating hand tools (pneumatic chipping hammers and grinders) while on the job. A physician on the research team who had extensive experience in the diagnosis of vibration syndrome examined each worker. Neither the workers nor the physician was told if a worker was classified as exposed or control. No workers in the control group were found to have vibration syndrome, while 83% of the exposed workers in the foundries and 64% of the exposed shipyard workers had discernable symptoms. Based on this study, what is the strongest claim the researchers can make about vibrating hand tools and vibration syndrome? Explain.

6. To determine if a new drug reduces blood cholesterol levels, researchers randomly select 1000 people with high blood cholesterol levels. The subjects are randomly assigned to the control group or the treatment group. The 500 subjects in the control group receive an injection of a harmless saline solution, while the 500 subjects in the treatment group receive an injection of the new drug. The researchers then monitor the blood cholesterol levels of the subjects over the next 6 weeks. If the blood cholesterol levels of the subjects in the control group remain unchanged while the blood cholesterol levels of all of the subjects in the treatment group decrease, what can the researchers claim? Explain.

7. To test the effectiveness of a new drug that prevents humans from contracting malaria, researchers randomly select 3000 people living in a malaria-endemic region who tested negative for malaria and do not take any drugs to prevent malaria. For the study, 1000 subjects are randomly assigned to the control group, 1000 to one treatment group, and 1000 to a second treatment group. For 6 months, health workers visit each subject once a week, give the subject a pill from a package prepared for that subject, and watch the subject swallow the pill. The subjects in the control group take placebos. The subjects in one of the treatment groups take pills containing the drug currently used to prevent malaria, while the subjects in the other treatment group take pills containing the new drug. The three types of pills all look alike. Neither the subjects nor the health workers know who receives which type of pill. The health workers record the number of subjects who contract malaria over the 6-month period.

a. Describe results that would support a claim that the new drug is more effective than both the drug currently used to prevent malaria and no drug.

b. Describe results that would support a claim that the new drug is less effective than the drug currently used to prevent malaria, but more effective than no drug.

c. This study is designed to try to control as many variables as possible, but it is impossible to control all the variables. Describe a variable that could affect the results of this experiment.

The student will describe events as subsets of a sample space, or as unions, intersections, or complements.

SELECTED RESPONSE

Two fair number cubes are rolled. Match each event with the correct subset of the sample space.

_____ 1. The first number is less than 3 and the second number is even.

_____ 2. The first number minus the second number equals 2.

_____ 3. The sum of the numbers is greater than 7.

_____ 4. The product of the numbers is an even number greater than 10.

A {(3, 1), (4, 2), (5, 3), (6, 4)}

B {(1, 2), (1, 4), (1, 6), (2, 2), (2, 4), (2, 6)}

C {(2, 6), (3, 4), (3, 6), (4, 3), (4, 4) (4, 5), (4, 6), (5, 4), (5, 6), (6, 2), (6, 3), (6, 4), (6, 5), (6, 6)}

D {(4, 2), (4, 4), (4, 6), (5, 2), (5, 4), (5, 6), (6, 2), (6, 4), (6, 6)}

E {(2, 5), (5, 2)}

F {(1, 6), (2, 5), (3, 4), (4, 3), (5, 2), (6, 1)}

G {(2, 6), (3, 5), (3, 6), (4, 4), (4, 5), (4, 6), (5, 3), (5, 4), (5, 5), (5, 6), (6, 2), (6, 3), (6, 4), (6, 5), (6, 6)}

H {(3, 1), (4, 2), (4, 1), (5, 3), (5, 2), (5, 1), (6, 4), (6, 3), (6, 2), (6, 1)}

Select the correct answer.

5. You spin a spinner with 8 equally likely landing spaces numbered 1 to 8. Event A is landing on a prime number. Event B is landing on an odd number. What is the intersection of A and B?

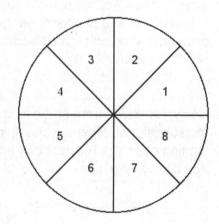

Ⓐ ∅

Ⓑ {3, 5, 7}

Ⓒ {1, 2, 3, 5, 7}

Ⓓ {1, 2, 3, 4, 5, 6, 7, 8}

6. Circle the expression that makes a true statement.

A group of 50 mice is being used in an experiment. Event A is a male mouse being chosen at random. Event B is a mouse that is at least 6 months old being chosen. Given that the notation ∩ means "intersection," and the notation ∪ means "union", the expression that describes a female mouse that is younger than 6 months old being chosen

is
$$A \cap B$$
$$A^c \cap B^c$$
$$A^c \cup B^c$$
$$A \cap B^c$$
.

CONSTRUCTED RESPONSE

7. Two fair coins are flipped and a fair number cube is rolled. What is the sample space of possible outcomes? Find the subset of the sample space that represents the results of the coin flips being different and rolling a number that is not prime.

_____

_____

8. A bag contains red marbles, yellow marbles, and blue marbles. Event *A* is picking a red marble, event *B* is picking a yellow marble, and event *C* is picking a blue marble. Describe each of the following scenarios using an intersection, a union, or a complement.

   a. Picking a single marble that is both red and yellow.

   _____

   b. Picking a single marble that is red or blue.

   _____

   c. Picking a marble that is not red and not blue.

   _____

   d. Are each of these scenarios possible? Explain.

   _____

9. The whole numbers from 1 to 10 are printed on two sets of cards, one red and one blue. You randomly pick one card from each set.

   a. Find the subset *A* of the sample space that represents picking two cards with the same number.

   _____

   b. Find the subset *B* of the sample space that represents picking two prime numbers.

   _____

   c. Describe the subset *C* of the sample space that represents picking two cards with the same prime number in terms of subsets *A* and *B*. Then find the elements of *C*.

   _____

   _____

10. Anna and Sanjay are playing a board game with the spinner shown below. Each section of the spinner has a number (1, 2, 3, 4) and a color (R = Red, Y = Yellow, G = Green, B = Blue).

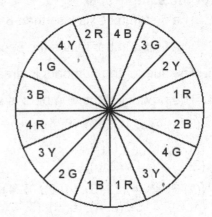

   a. What subset *A* of the sample space describes the spinner landing on a green section?

   _____

   b. What subset *B* of the sample space describes the spinner landing on a section with the number 2?

   _____

   c. What subset *C* of the sample space, in terms of *A* and *B*, describes the spinner landing on a green section with the number 2?

   _____

   d. Use your results from part c to find the subset that describes the spinner landing on any particular color and number combination.

   _____

   _____

   e. Which of the sets described in part d are empty?

   _____

   _____

The student will understand the definition of independent events and determine if events are independent.

SELECTED RESPONSE

1. Put a check mark in the column that describes the two events.

	Independent	Not Independent
Drawing two cards from a standard deck of cards that are both aces		
Rolling a fair number cube twice and getting 6 on both rolls		
Flipping a fair coin twice and getting heads on both flips		
Rolling a 3 on a fair number cube and flipping tails on a fair coin		

Select all correct answers.

2. A spinner numbered 1 through 6 has sections that are red, yellow, and blue. Juan spins the spinner 50 times and records the results in the table below. According to the data, which events are independent?

	Even	Odd	Total
Red	6	9	15
Yellow	7	8	15
Blue	7	13	20
Total	20	30	50

Ⓐ Landing on a red section and landing on an even number

Ⓑ Landing on a yellow section and landing on an even number

Ⓒ Landing on a blue section and landing on an even number

Ⓓ Landing on a red section and landing on an odd number

Ⓔ Landing on a yellow section and landing on an odd number

Ⓕ Landing on a blue section and landing on an odd number

Select the correct answer.

3. For two independent events A and B, $P(A) = 0.5$ and $P(B) = 0.4$. What is $P(A \text{ and } B)$?

Ⓐ 0.1   Ⓒ 0.8

Ⓑ 0.2   Ⓓ 0.9

CONSTRUCTED RESPONSE

4. A fair number cube is rolled two times. Are the events that the first roll is an even number and the second roll is a 6 independent? Justify your answer using the sample space and the product of the probabilities of each event.

_____

_____

_____

5. Monica has a bag with 30 marbles: 5 of the marbles are blue and striped, 10 of the marbles are striped but not blue, and 5 of the marbles are blue but not striped. Use probability to decide if picking a blue marble and picking a marble that has stripes are independent events.

_____

_____

_____

6. There are 12 men, 5 boys, 11 women, and 6 girls entered in a raffle. If each person has only one raffle ticket, are the events of the raffle winner being male and an adult independent? Explain.

_____

_____

_____

_____

7. A population of 200 laboratory mice contains 120 white mice and 80 gray mice. Of the mice, 50 are male and 150 are female. If the events of selecting a male mouse and selecting a white mouse are independent, how many of the mice are white and male? Show your work.

_____

_____

_____

_____

8. Suppose a fair coin is flipped two times.

a. Describe the sample space for flipping a coin twice.

_____

_____

b. Let event A be the coin landing on heads on the first flip, and event B be the coin landing on heads on the second flip. Are events A and B independent? Use the sample space and probability to explain.

_____

_____

_____

c. Suppose the coin is flipped a third time, and let event C be the coin landing on heads. Are events A, B, and C independent? Explain.

_____

_____

_____

_____

9. Esther surveys 150 students in her school and records if they are right- or left-handed, and if they prefer art class or gym class.

	Art	Gym	Total
Right-handed	52	78	130
Left-handed	8	12	20
Total	60	90	150

a. According to the data, are being right-handed and preferring art class independent events? Explain.

_____

_____

_____

b. According to the data, are being left-handed and preferring art class independent events? Explain.

_____

_____

_____

c. According to the data, are being right-handed and preferring gym class independent events? Explain.

_____

_____

_____

d. According to the data, are being left-handed and preferring gym class independent events? Explain.

_____

_____

_____

Name _____ Date _____ Class_____

The student will understand conditional probability, and use it to interpret the independence of events *A* and *B*.

SELECTED RESPONSE

Select the correct answer.

1. In a bag of 20 candies, 12 are red and 15 have peanuts in them. If the events of picking a red candy and picking a candy with peanuts are independent, how many of the red candies have peanuts?

   Ⓐ 3

   Ⓑ 6

   Ⓒ 9

   Ⓓ 12

2. Suppose events *A* and *B* are independent, $P(A) = 0.75$, and $P(B) = 0.5$. What is $P(A \mid B)$, the probability of *A* given *B*?

   Ⓐ 0.25

   Ⓑ 0.375

   Ⓒ 0.5

   Ⓓ 0.75

Select all correct answers.

3. For two events *A* and *B*, circle each statement that must be true in order for *A* and *B* to be independent.

   $\dfrac{P(A \text{ and } B)}{P(B)} = P(A)$

   $\dfrac{P(A \text{ and } B)}{P(A)} = P(B)$

   $P(A \mid B) = P(B \mid A)$

   $P(A) = P(B)$

   $P(B) = 1 - P(A)$

   $P(A \text{ and } B) = P(A) \cdot P(B)$

CONSTRUCTED RESPONSE

4. In a standard deck of 52 playing cards, find the probability that a black card is a three. Is this the same as the probability that a three is a black card? Use conditional probability to justify your answer.

   _____

   _____

   _____

5. Yusef spins the spinner shown below. Are landing on an odd number and landing on a prime number independent events? Explain using conditional probability.

   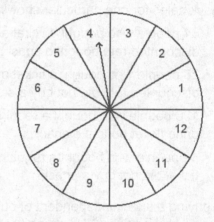

   _____

   _____

   _____

6. Events *A* and *B* are independent if $P(A \text{ and } B) = P(A) \cdot P(B)$. Use this fact to show that if events *A* and *B* are independent, $P(A \mid B) = P(A)$ and $P(B \mid A) = P(B)$.

   _____

   _____

   _____

7. A box contains 60 colored balls: 45 of the balls are purple, and 30 of the purple balls have stars on them. If a purple ball being randomly chosen and a ball with stars being randomly chosen are independent events, how many of the 60 colored balls have stars on them? Use conditional probability to justify your answer.

_____

_____

_____

_____

8. A movie theater tracks the ticket and snack sales for one particular showing.

   • 84 people who bought a ticket at a discounted rate bought a snack.

   • 28 people who bought a ticket at a discounted rate did not buy a snack.

   • 126 people who bought a regular price ticket bought a snack.

   • 42 people who bought a regular price ticket did not buy a snack.

   Is buying a snack independent of buying a regular price ticket? Use conditional probability to justify your answer.

_____

_____

_____

_____

_____

_____

9. Elena chooses one of 100 tiles numbered from 1 to 100. Let event A be the event that the number is even, let event B be the event that the number is a multiple of 5, and let event C be the event that the number is greater than 50. Find each probability.

   a. $P(A \mid B)$

   _____

   _____

   b. $P(B \mid A)$

   _____

   _____

   c. $P(A \mid C)$

   _____

   _____

   d. $P(C \mid A)$

   _____

   _____

   e. Are events A and B independent? Are events A and C independent? Explain.

   _____

   _____

   _____

   _____

   _____

   _____

   _____

The student will construct and interpret two-way frequency tables and use them to decide if events are independent.

SELECTED RESPONSE
Select the correct answer.

1. The table below shows the number of days that a meteorologist predicted it would be sunny, and the number of days it was sunny. Based on the data in the table, what is the conditional probability that it will be sunny on a day when the meteorologist predicts it will be sunny?

	Sunny	Not Sunny	Total
Predicts sunny	570	20	590
Does not predict sun	63	347	410
Total	633	367	1000

(A) 57%

(B) 59%

(C) 90%

(D) 97%

Select all correct answers.

2. Angela has a pack of 40 cards: some red, some blue, some with letters, and some with numbers. Based on the data shown in the table, which statements are true?

	Red	Blue	Total
Number	10	4	14
Letter	10	16	26
Total	20	20	40

(A) $P(\text{blue and number}) = \dfrac{1}{10}$

(B) $P(\text{red and letter}) = \dfrac{5}{13}$

(C) $P(\text{number | red}) = \dfrac{1}{2}$

(D) $P(\text{letter | blue}) = \dfrac{4}{5}$

(E) Picking a numbered card and picking a red card are independent events.

(F) Picking a lettered card and picking a blue card are independent events.

3. A bag contains green, orange, and purple balls, each numbered with a 1 or a 2. The table below shows how many of each kind of ball are in the bag.

	Number 1	Number 2	Total
Green	8	7	15
Orange	9	6	15
Purple	7	3	10
Total	24	16	40

Indicate whether each of the following is independent or not independent by putting a check mark in the appropriate column of the table.

	Independent	Not independent
Picking a green ball and a ball with a 1 on it		
Picking an orange ball and a ball with a 1 on it		
Picking a purple ball and a ball with a 1 on it		
Picking a green ball and a ball with a 2 on it		
Picking an orange ball and a ball with a 2 on it		
Picking a purple ball and a ball with a 2 on it		

CONSTRUCTED RESPONSE

4. Sandra is planning a dinner party for 100 people. Out of 45 men coming to the party, 36 ordered chicken. Out of the 55 women coming to the party, 24 ordered fish.

   a. Complete the two-way table below.

	Chicken	Fish	Total
Man	36		
Woman		24	
Total			

   b. What is the conditional probability that a guest who ordered fish is a man?

   _____

   c. What is the conditional probability that a guest who ordered chicken is a woman?

   _____

5. It is known that 3% of a population has a certain allergy. A test correctly identifies people with the allergy (positive result) 97% of the time. The test also correctly identifies people without the allergy (negative result) 94% of the time.

   a. The allergy test is given to 1000 people. Use the given information to fill in the table. Round to the nearest person.

	Allergy	No allergy	Total
Positive			
Negative			
Total	30		1000

   b. What is the probability that a person has the allergy if the person tests positive? Round to the nearest hundredth.

   _____

6. Manuela and Stephen survey 250 people at a sporting event and ask if they prefer hamburgers or hot dogs, and if they prefer regular or diet soda.

   - 90 people said they prefer hamburgers and regular soda.
   - 40 people said they prefer hamburgers and diet soda.
   - 70 people said they prefer hot dogs and regular soda.
   - 50 people said they prefer hot dogs and diet soda.

   a. Complete the table.

	Regular soda	Diet soda	Total
Hamburger			
Hot dog			
Total			250

   b. What is the probability that someone who prefers diet soda will also prefer hamburgers?

   _____

   c. What is the probability that someone who prefers hot dogs will also prefer regular soda?

   _____

   d. Are preferring diet soda and preferring hamburgers independent events? Explain.

   _____

   _____

   _____

   e. Are preferring regular soda and preferring hot dogs independent events? Explain.

   _____

   _____

   _____

Name _____ Date _____ Class_____

The student will recognize and explain the concepts of conditional probability and independence.

SELECTED RESPONSE
Select the correct answer.

1. 110 students are surveyed about their pets. The results are shown in the table. Which statement is true?

	Boys	Girls	Total
At least one pet	18	39	57
No pets	27	26	53
Total	45	65	110

Ⓐ 27% of the boys have no pets.

Ⓑ 40% of the boys have at least one pet.

Ⓒ 49% of the girls have no pets.

Ⓓ 57% of the students have at least one pet.

2. Circle the percent that makes a true statement.
In a bag of 60 candies, 36 are green and 45 have caramel in them. If the events of picking a green candy and picking a candy with caramel are independent, then the percent of the green candies that have caramel in them is

25%	75%
60%	100%

Select all correct answers.

3. Carl and Wendy are catering a party for 100 people. Out of the 45 men coming, 27 ordered chicken. Out of the 55 women coming, 33 ordered fish. Everyone ordered either chicken or fish. Which of the following are true?

Ⓐ 40% of the men ordered fish.

Ⓑ More than half of the people who ordered chicken are women.

Ⓒ The percent of men who ordered chicken is the same as the percent of women who ordered fish.

Ⓓ The probability that a person who ordered fish is a man is less than 33%.

Ⓔ The probability that a person who ordered chicken is a woman is less than 50%.

CONSTRUCTED RESPONSE

4. An allergy test is administered to 400 people. The results are shown in the table.

	Has allergy	Does not have allergy	Total
Test positive	10	19	29
Test negative	2	369	371
Total	12	388	400

a. What percent of test subjects who test positive have the allergy? Round to the nearest percent.

_____

b. What percent of test subjects who do not have the allergy test negative? Round to the nearest percent.

_____

5. A train station employee collects data on 160 incoming trains to the station. He notices that 18 of the 90 incoming trains on line A arrive late, and 14 of the 70 incoming trains on line B arrive late.

a. What is the probability that a train on line A arrives on time? What is the probability that any train arrives on time? Interpret your answers in the context of the situation.

_____

_____

b. Can you conclude that a train being on line A and a train arriving on time are independent events? Use your results from part a to explain your answer.

_____

_____

6. 250 students are surveyed about their after school activities. 125 students said they play basketball, and among those students, 55 said they also play soccer. What percent of the students who play basketball also play soccer? Show your work.

_____

_____

_____

7. A movie theater tracks the ticket and snack sales for one particular showing.

60 people who bought a ticket at a discounted price bought a snack.

36 people who bought a ticket at a discounted price did not buy a snack.

90 people who bought a ticket at the regular price bought a snack.

54 people who bought a ticket at the regular price did not buy a snack.

a. What is the probability that a person who bought a snack bought a ticket at the regular price? Show your work.

_____

_____

_____

b. Is the answer to part a the same as the probability that a person who bought a ticket at the regular price bought a snack? Explain.

_____

_____

_____

c. Interpret your answers from parts a and b in the context of the situation.

_____

_____

8. The two-way table below shows data about 85 students and their scores on a test. Sylvia claims that because 66 of the students got more than 6 hours of sleep and 20 of those students scored below 70%, about 30% of the students who scored below 70% got more than 6 hours of sleep.

	Below 70%	Above 70%	Total
Less than 6 hours	9	10	19
More than 6 hours	20	46	66
Total	29	56	85

a. What mistake did Sylvia make?

_____

_____

b. What is the correct probability that a student who scored below 70% got more than 6 hours of sleep?

_____

9. It is known that 2% of all mice in a laboratory have a genetic mutation. A scientist administers a test to 1000 mice. 95% of the mice that have the mutation have a positive test result, and 95% of the mice that do not have the mutation have a negative test result. Complete the two-way frequency table for the 1000 mice. Then use the table to find what percent of the mice that test positive have the mutation. Round to the nearest percent.

	Mutation	No mutation	Total
Test positive			
Test negative			
Total	20	980	1000

_____

_____

The student will find the conditional probability of *A* given *B* as the fraction of *B*'s outcomes that also belong to *A*.

SELECTED RESPONSE
Select the correct answer.

1. 200 people took part in a study involving a new headache medicine. After one week, the subjects were asked if they had a headache in the past week. According to the data in the two-way table, what fraction of the people who were given the placebo did not have a headache?

	Given medicine	Given placebo	Total
Headache	30	20	50
No headache	120	30	150
Total	150	50	200

Ⓐ $\frac{2}{5}$ Ⓒ $\frac{3}{5}$

Ⓑ $\frac{3}{4}$ Ⓓ $\frac{4}{5}$

2. Elena asks the students in one of her classes if they have a cat or a dog. Her results are recorded in the table below. What is the probability that a randomly selected student who has a cat will also have a dog?

	Dog	No dog	Total
Cat	5	8	13
No cat	15	4	19
Total	20	12	32

Ⓐ $\frac{1}{4}$ Ⓒ $\frac{5}{13}$

Ⓑ $\frac{5}{32}$ Ⓓ $\frac{8}{13}$

Select all correct answers.

3. Concession sales at a sporting event are monitored, and the data are recorded in the two-way table below. Which of the following statements are true?

	French fries	Onion rings	Total
Hamburger	252	144	396
Hot dog	216	108	324
Total	468	252	720

Ⓐ $\frac{7}{11}$ of the people who ordered a hamburger ordered French fries.

Ⓑ $\frac{4}{11}$ of the people who ordered French fries ordered a hamburger.

Ⓒ $\frac{3}{7}$ of the people who ordered a hamburger ordered onion rings.

Ⓓ $\frac{4}{7}$ of the people who ordered onion rings ordered a hamburger.

Ⓔ $\frac{6}{7}$ of the people who ordered a hot dog ordered French fries.

Ⓕ $\frac{2}{3}$ of the people who ordered French fries ordered a hot dog.

Ⓖ $\frac{1}{3}$ of the people who ordered a hot dog ordered onion rings.

Ⓗ $\frac{1}{2}$ of the people who ordered onion rings ordered a hot dog.

Match each conditional probability with the correct fraction.

	Male	Female	Total
Blue eyes	10	12	22
Brown eyes	38	44	82
Green eyes	12	14	26
Other eyes	20	30	50
Total	80	100	180

Using the list of fractions below Exercises 4–7, write the fraction that gives the indicated conditional probability.

4. The probability that a randomly selected male student has brown eyes.

5. The probability that a randomly selected female student has green eyes.

6. The probability that a randomly selected student with blue eyes is male.

7. The probability that a randomly selected student with green eyes is female.

$\dfrac{19}{41}$	$\dfrac{5}{11}$	$\dfrac{19}{40}$	$\dfrac{1}{8}$

$\dfrac{7}{50}$	$\dfrac{1}{6}$	$\dfrac{7}{26}$	$\dfrac{7}{13}$

CONSTRUCTED RESPONSE

8. Complete the two-way table below. Then find the fraction of red cards in a standard 52-card deck that have a number on them, and find the fraction of numbered cards that are red.

	Red	Black	Total
Number			
No number			
Total			52

9. Students in four of Ms. Peters's classes are surveyed about their favorite type of movie.

   Block A
   Action: 12, Comedy: 13, Drama: 6

   Block B
   Action: 9, Comedy: 11, Drama: 11

   Block C
   Action: 8, Comedy: 15, Drama: 7

   Block D
   Action: 11, Comedy: 4, Drama: 18

a. Complete the two-way table below to organize the data.

	A	B	C	D	Total
Action					
Comedy					
Drama					
Total					

b. What fraction of the students who prefer action movies are in Ms. Peters's block C class? Show your work.

_____

_____

c. What fraction of the students who are in Ms. Peters's block D class prefer dramas? Show your work.

_____

_____

d. What is the probability that a randomly selected student who is in Ms. Peters's block B class prefers comedies? What is the probability that a randomly selected student who prefers comedies is in Ms. Peters's block B class? Explain why the two probabilities are not the same.

_____

_____

The student will apply the Addition Rule of Probability, and interpret the answer in terms of the model.

SELECTED RESPONSE
Select all correct answers.

1. A bag contains 5 orange marbles, 7 green marbles, and 8 blue marbles, where 3 of the orange marbles have white stripes, 1 of the green marbles has white stripes, and 5 of the blue marbles have white stripes. Which of the following are true statements?

   (A) The probability that a randomly selected marble is orange or has white stripes is 0.85.

   (B) The probability that a randomly selected marble is orange or does not have white stripes is 0.7.

   (C) The probability that a randomly selected marble is green or has white stripes is 0.75.

   (D) The probability that a randomly selected marble is green or does not have white stripes is 0.6.

   (E) The probability that a randomly selected marble is blue or has white stripes is 0.25.

   (F) The probability that a randomly selected marble is blue or does not have white stripes is 0.375.

Select the correct answer.

2. A dodecahedral solid has 12 sides numbered 1 through 12, all equally likely to appear when you roll it. What is the likelihood that you roll an even number or a prime number?

   (A) It is impossible, because the probability is 0.

   (B) It is unlikely, because the probability is less than 0.5.

   (C) It is as likely as not, because the probability is about 0.5.

   (D) It is likely, because the probability is greater than 0.5.

3. Darren randomly chooses a card from a standard deck of 52 playing cards. What is the probability that Darren chooses a club or a queen?

   (A) $\dfrac{4}{52}$ (C) $\dfrac{16}{52}$

   (B) $\dfrac{13}{52}$ (D) $\dfrac{17}{52}$

4. Put a check mark in the column that describes the probability p for the outcome of the experiment described.

   A game show uses a fair spinner numbered 1 through 20.

	$p < 0.5$	$p = 0.5$	$p > 0.5$
A number less than 6 or a number greater than 15			
An odd number or a number greater than 5			
A multiple of 4 or a multiple of 6			
A multiple of 8 or a perfect square			
A prime number or a multiple of 3			

CONSTRUCTED RESPONSE

5. 16 cards numbered 1 through 16 are placed face down and Stephanie chooses one at random. What is the probability that the number on Stephanie's card is less than 5 or greater than 10? Show your work.

   _____

   _____

   _____

6. Joel rolls two fair number cubes at the same time. What is the probability that the sum of the numbers will be odd or less than 4? Show your work.

_____

_____

_____

7. A survey of a representative sample of 1000 employees at a company finds that 456 employees take the subway to work and 427 employees take a bus to work. Some employees have to take both the subway and a bus, and 310 employees take only a bus. Amanda says that the probability that a randomly selected employee takes the subway or a bus to work is $\frac{456}{1000} + \frac{427}{1000} = \frac{883}{1000} = 0.883$.

   a. Explain why Amanda's answer is incorrect.

   _____

   _____

   _____

   b. Use the addition rule to find the correct probability that a randomly selected employee takes the subway or a bus to work. Show your work.

   _____

   _____

   _____

   c. Calculate the probability that a randomly selected employee does not take the subway or a bus to get to work. Explain your reasoning.

   _____

   _____

   _____

8. A box contains 100 small rubber balls. The table below shows how many balls are red, how many are black, how many have stars, and how many do not have stars. What is the probability that a randomly selected ball is black or does not have stars on it? Justify your answer.

	Stars	No stars	Total
Red	0	65	65
Black	10	25	35
Total	10	90	100

_____

_____

9. The two-way table below shows data on the students at a college.

	Male	Female	Total
Freshman	1732	2258	3990
Sophomore	1720	2280	4000
Junior	1750	2350	4100
Senior	1726	2296	4022
Total	6928	9184	16,112

   a. Use the addition rule of probability to find the probability that a randomly selected student is a senior or female. Show your work.

   _____

   _____

   b. Use the addition rule of probability to find the probability that a randomly selected student is a junior or male. Show your work.

   _____

   _____

   c. Is it more likely that a randomly selected student is a senior or female, or that a randomly selected student is a junior or male? Explain.

   _____

   _____

   _____

The student will apply the Multiplication Rule of Probability, and interpret the answer.

SELECTED RESPONSE
Select the correct answer for each lettered part.

1. You have a set of 15 cards: 11 of the cards are white, 3 are red, and 1 is blue. You draw one card, set it aside, and draw a second card. For each combination of cards below, is there a less than 50% or greater than 50% chance of choosing those two cards?

   a. A white card, and then a red card
   - ○ Less than 50%
   - ○ Greater than 50%

   b. A white card, and then a white card
   - ○ Less than 50%
   - ○ Greater than 50%

   c. A card that is not blue, and then a blue card
   - ○ Less than 50%
   - ○ Greater than 50%

   d. A red card, and then a blue card
   - ○ Less than 50%
   - ○ Greater than 50%

   e. A card that is not red, and then a card that is not red
   - ○ Less than 50%
   - ○ Greater than 50%

Select the correct answer.

2. There are 5 apples and 6 plums in a fruit bowl. Which statement is correct about the likelihood that you randomly choose two apples?

   (A) You are less likely than not to randomly choose two apples.

   (B) You are as likely as not to randomly choose two apples.

   (C) You are more likely than not to randomly choose two apples.

   (D) It is not possible to randomly choose two apples.

3. A bag contains 5 red marbles and 3 yellow marbles. What is the probability of randomly choosing a red marble, setting it aside, and then randomly choosing a yellow marble?

   (A) $\dfrac{3}{28}$ (C) $\dfrac{15}{56}$

   (B) $\dfrac{15}{64}$ (D) $\dfrac{5}{14}$

CONSTRUCTED RESPONSE

4. Lily and Miguel survey 46 students from grade 9, 42 students from grade 10, 54 students from grade 11, and 38 students from grade 12. When examining the results of their survey, Lily and Miguel choose two students randomly.

   a. What is the probability that the first student will be from grade 9 and the second student will be from grade 10? Show your work.

   _____

   _____

   _____

   b. What is the probability that the first student will be from grade 9 and the second student will also be from grade 9? Show your work.

   _____

   _____

   _____

   c. Which has a greater likelihood: the result from part a or the result from part b?

   _____

   _____

5. There are 15 boys and 16 girls in an English class. The teacher randomly chooses two students to read parts from a play. Is it more likely that the teacher will choose a boy followed by a girl or a girl followed by a boy? Use probability to explain your answer.

_____

_____

6. A board game has 5 tiles of each letter of the English alphabet, for a total of 130 tiles. These tiles are placed face down. Edwin incorrectly says that the probability of choosing a tile with a vowel (a, e, i, o, u) on it followed by another tile with a vowel on it is $\frac{5}{26} \cdot \frac{4}{25} = \frac{2}{65}$.

   a. What is the correct probability? Show your work.

   _____

   _____

   b. What error did Edwin make? For what different set of lettered tiles would Edwin's calculations correctly represent the probability of choosing a tile with a vowel on it followed by another tile with a vowel on it?

   _____

   _____

7. For a carnival game, 20 rubber ducks numbered 1 to 20 float in a large tub. To win the game, you must pick two ducks whose numbers add up to at least 30. How likely are you to pick the number 20 on your first pick and then win the game? Explain your answer.

   _____

   _____

   _____

8. The names of 4 boys and 6 girls are written on slips of paper and placed in a bowl. You take one slip of paper out of the bowl, set it aside, and then take another slip of paper.

   a. What is the probability that you choose a boy's name followed by a girl's name?

   _____

   b. Is the probability different if you put the first slip of paper back in the bowl before choosing the second slip of paper? Explain.

   _____

9. A cooler contains 12 ham sandwiches, 15 roast beef sandwiches, and 10 turkey sandwiches. Organize the following events from least likely to most likely. Use probability to justify your answer.

   (1) Randomly picking a ham sandwich, putting it aside, and randomly picking a roast beef sandwich

   (2) Randomly picking a ham sandwich, putting it aside, and randomly picking a turkey sandwich

   (3) Randomly picking a roast beef sandwich, putting it aside, and randomly picking a turkey sandwich

   (4) Randomly picking a ham sandwich, putting it aside, and randomly picking a ham sandwich

   (5) Randomly picking a roast beef sandwich, putting it aside, and randomly picking a roast beef sandwich

   (6) Randomly picking a turkey sandwich, putting it aside, and randomly picking a turkey sandwich

   _____

   _____

   _____

   _____

The student will use permutations and combinations to compute probabilities and solve problems.

SELECTED RESPONSE
Select the correct answer.

1. There are 12 players on a baseball team. In how many different ways can the coach choose players for left field, right field, and center field?

   (A) 36

   (B) 220

   (C) 1320

   (D) 1728

2. There are 8 runners in a race. What is the probability that Abby, Becca, and Carmen place first, second, and third in any order?

   (A) $\dfrac{1}{336}$

   (B) $\dfrac{1}{56}$

   (C) $\dfrac{3}{28}$

   (D) $\dfrac{3}{8}$

Select all correct answers.

3. Suppose 2 cards are drawn at random from a standard deck of 52 cards. Which expressions below represent the probability that both cards are aces?

   (A) $\dfrac{_4C_2}{_{52}C_2}$

   (B) $\dfrac{_{52}C_2}{_4C_2}$

   (C) $\dfrac{1}{_4C_2}$

   (D) $\dfrac{1}{221}$

   (E) $\dfrac{1}{2652}$

CONSTRUCTED RESPONSE

4. At summer camp, Tina can choose any three of the following activities.

   Archery, Painting, Pottery, Swimming, Sailing, Soccer

   Use permutations to find the probability that Tina chooses archery, pottery, and swimming in that order. Show your work.

   _____

5. A bank assigns random 4-digit numbers for ATM access codes. In each code, no digit is repeated. Use combinations to find the number of ways that 4 digits can be chosen from 10 digits if order is not important. What is the probability that Edmond is assigned a code with the digits 6, 7, 8, and 9 in any order? Show your work.

   _____

6. A bag contains 10 tiles with the letters A, B, C, D, E, F, G, H, I, and J. Five tiles are chosen and placed in a row. Meghan says that the probability of the five tiles spelling FACED is $\dfrac{1}{252}$. Her work is shown below.

   Let S be the sample space and let A be the event that the tiles spell FACED.

   $n(S) = {}_{10}P_5 = \dfrac{10!}{(10-5)!} = 30,240$

   $n(A) = {}_5P_5 = \dfrac{5!}{(5-5)!} = 120$

   So, $P(A) = \dfrac{n(A)}{n(S)} = \dfrac{120}{30,240} = \dfrac{1}{252}$.

   What was Meghan's error? What is the correct probability of the five tiles spelling FACED? Show your work.

   _____

7. There are 6 boys and 7 girls on student council. The principal randomly chooses 4 students to meet with the head of the school committee.

   a. Use a combination to find the number of ways that the principal could randomly choose 4 students. Show your work.

_____

_____

_____

   b. Use a combination to find the number of ways that the principal could randomly choose 4 girls. Show your work.

_____

_____

_____

   c. Use your answers from parts a and b to find the probability that the principal chooses all girls to meet with the head of the school committee.

_____

_____

_____

   d. Is the principal more likely to choose all girls or all boys? Explain.

_____

_____

_____

8. The 10 members of the math club want to choose a president, a vice-president, and a treasurer. Matt, Cho, and Erin are all members of the math club.

   a. What is the probability that Matt is chosen to be the president, Cho is chosen to be the vice-president, and Erin is chosen to be the treasurer? Use permutations in your answer.

_____

_____

   b. What is the probability that Matt, Cho, and Erin are chosen to fill the three positions in any order? Use combinations in your answer.

_____

_____

   c. Are your answers from parts a and b the same? Explain.

_____

_____

_____

9. Travis's collection of DVDs contains 14 comedies, 12 dramas, and 10 action movies. Use combinations to find the probability of each of the following compound events, and then order the events A, B, C, and D from least likely to most likely.

Event A: Randomly selecting 3 comedies

Event B: Randomly selecting 3 dramas

Event C: Randomly selecting 3 action movies

Event D: Randomly selecting 3 movies that are not dramas

_____

_____

_____

The student will use probability to make fair decisions.

SELECTED RESPONSE

Select the correct answer.

1. While watching scary movies one night, 8 friends hear a loud noise in the basement. They decide that they all should go to investigate the noise. Which of these describe a fair method to determine who goes down the basement stairs first?

   Ⓐ Have the friends take turns flipping a coin. The first friend to get heads goes first.

   Ⓑ Assign a number to each friend and roll a fair number cube to select one.

   Ⓒ Assign a different outcome for flipping a coin 3 times to each friend and flip a coin 3 times.

   Ⓓ Have the friends take turns flipping a coin twice. The first friend to get two heads goes first.

2. Suzi, Dmitri, and 11 of their classmates are playing a game. The game will have a single winner. If the game is fair, what is the probability that NEITHER Dmitri nor Suzi wins?

   Ⓐ $\dfrac{2}{13}$ Ⓒ $\dfrac{2}{11}$

   Ⓑ $\dfrac{11}{13}$ Ⓓ $\dfrac{9}{11}$

Select all correct answers.

3. If 2 fair number cubes are rolled and the sum of the numbers facing up is used to select a person from a group of 4, for which of these assignments of sums is the selection process fair?

   Ⓐ {2, 3, 10, 11, 12}; {4, 7}; {5, 6}; {8, 9}

   Ⓑ {2, 3, 4}; {5, 6}; {7, 8, 9}; {10, 11, 12}

   Ⓒ {2, 6, 10}; {3, 4, 5}; {7, 11, 12}; {8, 9}

   Ⓓ {2, 4, 6}; {3, 7, 12}; {5, 8}; {9, 10, 11}

   Ⓔ {2, 3, 4, 10}; {5, 6, 7}; {8, 11}; {9, 12}

   Ⓕ {2, 3, 7}; {4, 5, 11}; {6, 8, 12}; {9, 10, 11}

CONSTRUCTED RESPONSE

4. Mandy and 5 of her friends are playing a board game. One of the friends argues that the game is not fair because they have played 7 times and he has yet to win. If the game is actually fair, what is the probability of not winning 7 games in a row? If necessary, round your answer to the nearest tenth of a percent.

   _____

5. Each spinner shown is divided into equal sections. In a game, 4 players take turns spinning both spinners and finding the sum of the results. Player A wins if the sum is 2, 6, or 10, player B wins if the sum is 3 or 5, player C wins if the sum is 4 or 8, and player D wins otherwise. Is this game fair? Explain why or why not.

   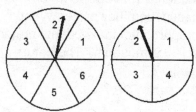

   _____

6. The spinner shown is divided into equal sections. In a game, 2 players each spin the spinner and record the sum of the results. Player A wins if the sum is even, and player B wins if the sum is odd. Show that this game is fair. Describe another way to assign the sums to the players that results in a fair game.

   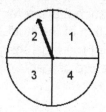

   _____

7. There are 30 students in a 4th grade class. The teacher is planning a class trip to either the science museum or the nature center. The table shows the arrangement of the students' desks in the classroom, along with a number to identify each student and a letter to indicate which destination the student would prefer (S for the science museum or N for the nature center).

Row 1	1	2	3	4	5	6
	S	S	S	N	S	S
Row 2	7	8	9	10	11	12
	N	N	S	N	S	N
Row 3	13	14	15	16	17	18
	N	N	S	N	N	S
Row 4	19	20	21	22	23	24
	S	S	N	N	N	N
Row 5	25	26	27	28	29	30
	N	S	N	N	N	N

a. Suppose the teacher asks all the students in the class which destination they prefer. What proportion of the students prefer the science museum? The nature center?

b. Suppose the teacher asks only the students in row 1 which destination they prefer. What proportion of the students in the sample prefer the science museum? The nature center?

c. Suppose the teacher asks a random sample of only 6 students—students 4, 12, 14, 19, 25, and 28—which destination they prefer. What proportion of the students in the sample prefer the science museum? The nature center?

d. Assuming one of the methods described in parts a, b, and c is to be used to decide the destination, rank the methods in order of fairness. Explain.

8. Stephan and Nariam help a neighbor stack her firewood and receive a bag of jelly beans as a thank-you gift. To decide who gets the bag of jelly beans, they play a game with the following rules:

• They take turns tossing a fair coin.

• When the coin lands heads up, Stephan gets a point.

• When the coin lands tails up, Nariam gets a point.

• The first player to reach 10 points wins the game and gets the bag of jelly beans.

After the tossing the coin 14 times, the score is tied at 7 points each. Stephan and Nariam are bored with the game and decide to evenly divide the jelly beans. Complete the following parts to show that this decision is fair.

a. Determine the maximum number of tosses that would have been needed to finish the game, and list the sample space for these tosses.

b. In how many of the outcomes from part a would Stephan have won? How many would Nariam have won? Notice that if one of the players wins after only 3 or 4 tosses, continuing to play for 5 tosses does not change who wins.

c. Explain how the results from part b show that the decision to evenly divide the jelly beans is fair.

The student will analyze decisions and strategies using probability concepts.

SELECTED RESPONSE
Select the correct answer.

1. A baseball team is losing by one run in the bottom half of the final inning of a game. There is one out and a runner on third. If the next batter hits a sacrifice fly, then the runner on third will score. If the next batter hits a home run, then the batting team wins. If the next batter strikes out, the runner on third does not score. The manager of this team has two pinch-hitters available. The table below shows some of the past results when the manager used these hitters in similar situations. Based on the data, which of the following statements is true?

	Batter A	Batter B	Total
Hits a home run	12	9	21
Hits a sacrifice fly	30	19	49
Strikes out	18	12	30
Total	60	40	100

Ⓐ If the manager wants to at least tie the game with the next batter, batter A is a better choice than batter B.

Ⓑ If the manager wants to at least tie the game with the next batter, batter B is a better choice than batter A.

Ⓒ If the manager wants to win the game with the next batter, batter A is a better choice than batter B.

Ⓓ If the manager wants to win the game with the next batter, batter B is a better choice than batter A.

Select all correct answers.

2. A supermarket gets 50% of its apples from farmer A, 35% of its apples from farmer B, and 15% of its apples from farmer C. From experience, the supermarket manager knows that 2% of apples from farmer A arrive rotten, 4% of apples from farmer B arrive rotten, and 6% of apples from farmer C arrive rotten. Which are good decisions?

Ⓐ The manager selects an apple at random, finds it is rotten, and concludes it most likely came from farmer A.

Ⓑ The manager selects an apple at random, finds it is good, and concludes it most likely came from farmer A.

Ⓒ The manager selects an apple at random, finds it is rotten, and concludes it most likely came from farmer B.

Ⓓ The manager selects an apple at random, finds it is good, and concludes it least likely came from farmer B.

Ⓔ The manager selects an apple at random, finds it is rotten, and concludes it least likely came from farmer C.

Ⓕ The manager selects an apple at random, finds it is good, and concludes it least likely came from farmer C.

CONSTRUCTED RESPONSE

3. A vaccine is 95% effective in preventing a serious disease, but the vaccine has a 2% chance of causing a serious allergic reaction. If unvaccinated people have a 10% chance of contracting the disease, is it better to risk the disease or the vaccine? Explain.

_____

4. There is 1 minute remaining in an ice hockey game and the road team is behind by 1 goal. The coach of the road team is considering replacing the goaltender with another offensive player. Historically in ice hockey, the road team scores a goal every 28.6 minutes when both teams have goaltenders on the ice. The probability that the road team scores a goal changes when the road team replaces the goaltender. Furthermore, the probability that the home team loses a player due to a penalty increases when the road team replaces the goaltender, which also changes the probability that the road team scores a goal. The two-way frequency table shows the distribution of a population of 10,000 minutes of play when the goaltender is replaced. Use the table to help determine what the road team coach should do to maximize the probability that the road team scores a goal. Show your work. Notice that since the home team is already leading, there is no need to consider the probability that the home team scores during the final minute.

	No penalty	Penalty	Total
Goal	885	490	1375
No goal	6615	2010	8625
Total	7500	2500	10,000

5. It is estimated that 0.5% of a population has a particular virus. There are two tests for this virus. Test A correctly identifies someone who has the virus 97% of the time and correctly identifies someone who does not have the virus 97% of the time. Test B correctly identifies someone who has the virus 99% of the time and correctly identifies someone who does not have the virus 95% of the time.

a. For each test, what percent of the people who test positive actually do not have the virus? Show your work, and round to the nearest percent.

_____

b. For each test, what percent of the people who test negative actually do have the virus? Show your work, and round to the nearest percent.

_____

c. If the virus is very contagious, which test would be better to prevent infected people from spreading the virus? Use parts a and b to explain.

_____

d. If the side effects of the medicine used to fight the virus are substantial, which test would be better to avoid treating people who don't need to be treated? Use parts a and b to explain.

_____

6. A company manufactures office furniture. During a board meeting one day, the chair that the president of the company is using breaks. Since the company manufactured the chair, the president is furious and calls the quality manager into the meeting to find out which parts supplier is responsible for this humiliating defect. The company uses three suppliers for the part that broke. Supplier A provides that part 20% of the time, supplier B 30% of the time, and supplier C the remainder. Results from continuous random sampling show that on average, 3% of parts from supplier A, 2.5% of parts from supplier B, and 1% of parts from supplier C are defective. Use this information to find the probability that a defective part is from each supplier. Which supplier is most likely responsible for the defective part? Show your work.

_____